Guitar Lessons

&

Music Theory

Bundle

Teach Yourself How to Play Guitar and Read Sheet Music, Theory & Technique. 2 Books in 1

by Woody Morgan

GUITAR LESSONS

FOR BEGINNERS

be considered liable in any fashion for any damages or hardships that may result from any of the information talked about this.

Additionally, the information in the accompanying pages is planned distinctly for informational purposes and should, in this manner, be thought of as universal. As befitting its nature, it is introduced without assurance regarding its drawn-out validity or break quality. Trademarks that are referenced are managed without composed consent and can not the slightest bit be viewed as underwriting from the trademark holder.

TABLE OF CONTENTS

INTRODUCTION

Numerous beginner guitarists surrender in the after attempting a couple of chords, especially chords that are not for beginners. Some will wrongly study the chords of their main tunes rapidly and then get disappointed because the chords are excessively hard. When figuring out how to play the guitar, it is ideal to play open chords first, and then practice speedy harmony changes and playing to a mood before trying to play a song.

In an open harmony, each finger compares to one string to the press. In a barre harmony, one finger may push on a few strings all the while. It is ideal for examining barre chords simply in the wake of mastering the essential open chords. This book instructs chords that are anything but difficult to play, yet enough to go with numerous songs. This fills in as a guide on what chords ought to be concentrated by the beginner guitarist. Figuring out how to play the guitar requires tolerance. The main mystery of mastering guitars lies in ordinary practice.

Getting Ready

Notes and chords

Beginners don't have to consider music theory to play guitars; however, having some basic information would help. An essential understanding of notes and chords is strongly suggested, however. At the point when a solitary guitar string is culled, the sound heard compares to a musical note. A harmonic arrangement of notes is a harmony. A harmony movement fills in as support tracks to a song. An outlined guide that shows what strings to press and where to squeeze them is referred to as a harmony graph or a harmony chart. A-B-C-D-E F-G-A-B-C-D-E-F-G ...

All learners must remember the above letters of the letter set. They speak to both the notes and the chords accessible to the guitarists. Those familiar with Do-Re-Mi can utilize the accompanying as a guide; however, it isn't required when figuring out how to play guitar.

C – Do D – Re E - Mi F - Fa G - So A - La B – Ti A sharp after the letter (#) relates to a half note higher. On the off chance that in note C, at that point C# is the note among C and D. A flat (b) is a half note lower.

If in the note D, at that point Db is the note among C and D. Note that C# and Db relate to a similar harmony. All notes and chords have a half note or harmony in the middle of, aside from be-tween B and C, just as among E and F. This implies there are no B# and Cb just as E# and Fb.

Here is the successive rundown of notes and chords. C-C#-D-D#-E-F-F#-G-G#-An A#-BC, another symbol in this book, is the minor sign spoke to by the little letter "m." For instance, the letter C speaks to the C major harmony or read as just C harmony, while Cm peruses as C minor harmony.

Tuning the guitar

A standard guitar has six strings extended from the headstock to the bridge. Electric guitar strings have three injured strings speaking to the lower notes, while acoustic guitar strings have four injured strings. The base, unwounded string, will be string #1 while the top, the injured string, will be string #6. Observe the string numbers while changing guitar strings. E A D G B E When the strings are open (not squeezed), culling the strings start to finish will produce the note E A D G B E in an arrangement, if they are in order. All guitarists ought to have a guitar tuner. Watch that all strings are in order before beginning any training. A little tuner that cuts on the head-stock will do. Start by tuning string #6. Pluck the 6th string and turn the machine head until the tuner shows an E. Utilize the succession C-C#-D-D#-E-F-F#-G-G#-An A#-BC as a manual to decide whether the showed note is excessively high or excessively low. Do likewise for different strings utilizing the table underneath as a tuning guide. E – string #6– string #5 D – string #4 G – string #3 B – string #2 E – string #1

How to peruse a harmony diagram

Hold the guitar with the fretboard in front and the tummy laying on your lap. The injured strings on the left relate to the furthest left vertical lines on the harmony diagram, while the unwounded strings on the privilege speak to the furthest right vertical lines on the graph. The vertical lines on the harmony diagram speak to the strings 6-5-4-3-2-1 read from left to right. On the off chance that no string is squeezed (no dark spots on the diagram), it compares to the notes E-A-D-G-B-E read from left to right. All guitarists ought to remember this arrangement.

The level lines speak to the frets wires on the guitar. The space over the first flat line compares to the principal fret of the guitar. A number to one side of the diagram, whenever appeared, demonstrates the fret number whenever appeared. The highest fret on the guitar is fret number 1. For a right-handed guitarist, #1 – forefinger #2 – center finger #3 – ring finger

#4 – pinky finger Legend X – don't press or pluck O – pluck without squeezing the string (open string).

The numbers on the graph show what finger to utilize when pushing on the relating string of the guitar. Assuming more than two strings have a similar number, at that point, it is a barre harmony. This implies the doled out finger (typically finger #1) lays on the stamped strings on the assigned fret. Beginner guitarists need not stress over barre chords until they are calm, playing open chords.

Holding the pick and playing

Hold the pick between the thumb and the side of the pointing finger, with the long side of the pick opposite to the thumb. Without the palm touching the strings, let the pick slide over the strings with a descending movement close the sound hole. For the time being, playing will comprise of descending strokes.

CHAPTER 01

UNDERSTANDING YOUR GUITAR

T o reach guitar mastery, we will start from the earliest starting point, which is understanding the components of your guitar.

Components of a guitar

Playing the guitar isn't as troublesome as it appears; be that as it may, because a guitar has a few components, the errand can get confounding and appear to be overwhelming. By finding out about the different components of a guitar, you will figure out how to hold it all the more easily and play it with certainty. To begin us off, how about we understand the various kinds of guitars.

Varieties of Guitar

There are two main sorts of guitars, acoustic and electric; both have a wooden and metal body separately. Commonality with any instrument is important; hence, let us depict in detail what a guitar resembles and what work every one of its parts performs.

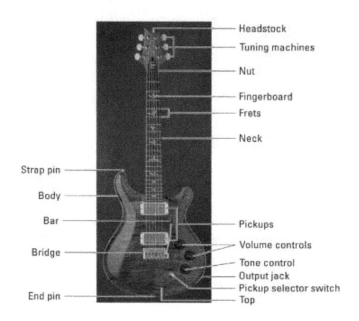

Image 1

The Elements of A Guitar

1. Back (acoustic just): The piece of the body that holds the sides in place; made from a few bits of wood.

2. Bar (electric just): On certain models, a metal bar joined to the bridge that changes the string pressure by tilting the bridge to and from. Additionally, called the tremolo bar, whammy bar, vibrato bar, and wang bar.

3. Body: The container that gives a stay to the neck and bridge and makes the playing surface for the correct hand. On an acoustic, the body incorporates the intensifying sound chamber that produces the guitar's tone. On an electric, it comprises of the lodging for the bridge get together and gadgets (pickups just as volume and tone controls).

6

4. Bridge: The metal (electric) or wood (acoustic) plate that and chords the strings to the body.

5. Bridge pins (acoustic just): Plastic or wooden dowels that embed through bridge openings and hold the strings safely to the bridge.

6. End pin: A post where the backside of the lash interfaces. On acoustic-electrics (acoustic guitars with worked in pickups and gadgets), the pin regularly serves as the yield jack where you plugin.

7. Fingerboard: Fingerboard: A flat, plank like bit of wood that sits on the neck, where you position your left-hand fingers to play notes and chords. The fingerboard is otherwise called the fretboard since the frets are installed in it.

8. Frets: (1) Thin metal wires or bars are running opposite to the strings that shorten the vibrating length of a string, empowering it to produce various pitches.

9. Headstock: The area that holds the tuning machines (hard-product gathering) and gives a spot to the producer to show its logo. Not to be mistaken for "Woodstock," which was the area of New York that gave a spot to the '60s age to show its music.

10. Neck: The long, club like wooden piece that interfaces the head-stock to the body.

11. Nut: A furrowed bit of hardened nylon or other manufactured substance that prevents the strings from vibrating past the neck. The strings go through the notches on their way to the tuning machines in the headstock. The nut is one of the two focuses at

which the vibrating zone of the string closes. (The other is the bridge.)

12. Output jack (electric just): The inclusion points for the string that associates the guitar to an intensifier or other electronic gadget.

13. Pickup selector (electric just): A switch that figures out which pickups are as of now dynamic.

14. Pickups (electric just): Barlike magnets that make the electrical current, which the speaker changes over into musical sound.

15. Saddle: For acoustic, a flimsy plastic strip that sits inside a space in the bridge; for electric, separate metal parts that give the contact point to the strings and the bridge.

16. Sides (acoustic just): Separate bent wooden pieces on the body that combine the top to the back.

17. Strap pin: The metal post in which the front, or top, finish of the lash associates. (Note: Not all acoustics have a lash pin. On the off chance that the guitar is missing one, tie the highest point of the tie around the headstock.)

18. Strings: The six metal (which for electric and steel-string acoustic guitars) or nylon (for old-style guitars) wires that, drawn tight, produce the notes of the guitar. Although not carefully the part of the actual guitar (you append and evacuate them voluntarily on the guitar), strings are a vital piece of the entire framework, and a guitar's whole plan and structure spin around making the strings ring out with a happy clamor.

19. Top: The face of the guitar. On an acoustic, this piece is additionally the sounding board, which produces practically all the guitar's acoustic characteristics. On an electric, the top is only a corrective or improving top that overlays the remainder of the body material.

20. Tuning machines: Geared components that raise and lower the pressure of the strings, attracting them to various pitches. The string wraps firmly around a post that sticks out through the top or face of the headstock. The post goes through to the rear of the headstock, where apparatuses associate it to a tuning key. Otherwise called tuners, tuning pegs, tuning keys, and tuning gears.

21. Volume and tone controls (electric just): Knobs that change the uproar of the guitar's sound and its bass and treble frequencies.

How Guitars Make Sound

After you can perceive the fundamental pieces of the guitar, you may likewise need to understand how those parts cooperate to make a sound (on the off chance that you happen to pick the Parts of a Guitar classification in Jeopardy! or, on the other hand, get into an overwhelming contention with another guitarist about string vibration and string length). We present this data in the accompanying areas to make sure you know why your guitar sounds how it does, rather than like a kazoo or an accordion. The significant thing to recall is that a guitar makes the sound; however, you make the music.

Strings doing their thing

Any instrument must have some piece of it moving in a standard, rehashed movement to produce musical sound (a continuous pitch, or tone). In a guitar, this part is the vibrating string. A string that you bring to a specific pressure and then set moving (by a culling activity) produces an anticipated sound for instance, the note A. When you tune a string of your guitar to many pressures, you get various tones. The more noteworthy the strain of a string, the higher the pitch.

Of course, it would be difficult to adjust the pressure that is applied to each string. So, guitarists resort to the next method to change a string's pitch by shortening its compelling vibrating length. They do as such by worrying pacing to and from.

In guitar-talk, worrying alludes to pushing the string against the fretboard, so the string vibrates just between the fingered fret and the bridge. Therefore, by moving the left hand here and there the neck (close to the bridge and the nut, separately), you can change pitches serenely and without any problem. The way that littler instruments, for example, mandolins and violins, are higher in pitch than are cellos and basses (and guitars, so far as that is concerned) is no mishap.

Their pitch is higher because their strings are shorter. The string pressure of every one of these instruments might be firmly related, causing them to feel some-what reliable in light of the hands and fingers, however, the radical distinction in string lengths is the thing that outcomes in the wide contrasts of pitch among them.

Holding the Guitar

When it comes to learning fundamental guitar, nothing is as significant as realizing how to hold your guitar. Realizing how to hold your guitar incorporates your stance, hand situation, and sitting region. Let us talk about these angles. Wrongly holding your guitar can have serious ramifications on your wellbeing since it can cause back, shoulder, neck, arm, and wrist torment, just as different genuine conditions, for example, tendonitis, dull strain in-jury, and Carpel Tunnel Syndrome. All things considered, before you figure out how to play the guitar, get acquainted with withholding your guitar immediately.

Sitting Area

If you are just beginning, figure out how to hold the guitar while in a certain position, as stunning as it appears to play the guitar while in a standing position, it is difficult for a beginner to ace that style. Pick a hard-sponsored seat or a stool and ensure it has no armrests because to hold the guitar easily, you need an open space for your arms. Besides, the tallness of the seat or stool ought to be to such an extent that your knees structure a correct edge and the two feet should contact the ground, so you can undoubtedly lay the guitar on your thigh without it sneaking off.

Stance

When you are in a situated position, ensure your back is straight, and you are not slouching forward. For the midsection of the guitar to lay on your thigh, utilize a little stool or box to lift your prevailing leg marginally higher than your other leg. Try not to lift your leg on your toes since that can be awkward and tedious.

Guitar Placement

When you are comfortable in your seat, get your guitar and spot the midriff of your guitar, which is the bend on the guitar's body, to your right side or predominant thigh. The rear of the guitar should lean against your stomach and chest while the neck of the guitar should point somewhat upwards. To understand this, guarantee the thickest string on your guitar focuses on the roof, during the slenderest towards the floor. If you are correct handed, your correct arm should make sure about the body of the guitar between your elbow and lower arm, while your wrist should lay on the bridge. With your left hand, make a paw wherein to hold the neck of the guitar. To make a paw, just spot your thumb on the rear of your guitar's neck; your center finger should ascend as though copying a paw. With your forefinger, press the thickest string E, press the A string with your ring finger, and D string with your pinky finger. You currently have the hand procedure called the 'hook.'

Utilizing the left and right hands together

The guitar regularly requires two hands cooperating to make music. If you need to play, say, center C on the piano, everything you do is take your forefinger, position it over the proper white key under the piano's logo, and drop it down: donning. A preschooler can sound simply like Elton John if playing just center C, because only one finger of one hand, squeezing one key, makes the sound. The guitar is, to some degree, extraordinary. To play center C on the guitar, you should take your left-hand forefinger and fret the second string (that is, press it down to the fingerboard) at the first fret. This activity, however, doesn't produce any sound. You should then strike or pluck that second string with your

12

correct hand to produce the note center C perceptibly. Music perusers observe: The guitar sounds an octave lower than its composed notes. For instance, playing a composed, third-space C on the guitar produces a center C.

Notes on the neck: Half step and frets

The smallest interim (unit of musical separation in pitch) of the musical scale is the half advance. On the piano, the rotating white and dark keys speak to this interim (as do the spots where you discover two adjoining white keys with no dark key in the middle). To continue steps on a keyboard instrument significantly, you move your finger up or down to the following accessible key, white or dark. On the guitar, frets the even metal wires (or bars) that you see implanted in the fretboard, running opposite to the strings speak to these half advances. To go up or somewhere near half strides on a guitar intends to move your left hand each fret in turn, higher or lower on the neck.

Contrasting how acoustics and electrics produce sound

Vibrating strings produce the various tones on a guitar. Be that as it may, you should have the option to hear those tones or you face one of those "if-a-tree-falls-in-a-forest" questions. For an acoustic guitar, that is no issue, because an acoustic instrument gives its intensifier as the empty sound load that helps its sound well, acoustically. In any case, anelectric guitar makes practically no acoustic sound by any means. (All things considered, a minor piece, similar to a humming mosquito, yet not even close to enough to fill an arena or outrage your nearby neighbors.) An electric instrument makes its tones completely through electronic

1

methods. The vibrating string is as yet the wellspring of the sound, yet an empty wood chamber isn't what makes those vibrations discernible. Rather, the vibrations upset, or regulate, the attractive field that the pickups wire-wrapped magnets situated underneath the strings produce. As the vibrations of the strings adjust the pickup's attractive field, the pickup produces a little electric flow that precisely mirrors that tweak.

Guitars, in this way, make sound by intensifying string vibrations either acoustically (bypassing the sound waves through an empty chamber) or electronically (by enhancing and yielding a current through a speaker). That is the physical procedure anyway. How a guitar produces various sounds and the ones that you need it to make it up to you and how you coordinate the pitches that those strings perform. Left-hand worrying is what changes these pitches. Your right-hand movements produce the sound by getting the string underway, yet they likewise decide the musicality (the beat or heartbeat), rhythm (the speed of the music), and feel (translation, style, turn, enchantment, magic, jene sais quoi, whatever) of those pitches. Set up both hand movements, and they spell music make that guitar music

CHAPTER 02

HOW TO TUNE YOUR GUITAR

Tuning is to guitarists what equal stopping is to city drivers: a regular and important action that can be vexingly hard to ace. In contrast to the piano, which expert tunes and you never need to alter until whenever the expert tuner drops by, the guitar is regularly tuned by its owner, and it needs consistent modifying. One of the incredibly boring truths to face, is that before you can even play music on the guitar, you should persevere through the meticulous procedure of getting your instrument in order. Luckily for guitarists, you have just six strings to tune instead of the couple hundred strings in a piano. Likewise, reassuring is the way that you can utilize a few distinct strategies to get your guitar in order, as this part portrays.

Before You start: Strings and Frets by the Numbers: We're going to begin from the starting point, or for this situation, string one. Before you can tune your guitar, you have to realize how to allude to the two principle players strings and frets.

Strings: Strings are numbered successively 1 through 6. The first string is the skinniest, found nearest to the floor (when you hold the guitar in playing position). Stirring your way up, the sixth string is the fattest,

1

nearest to the roof. We suggest that you retain the letter names of the open strings (E, A, D, G, B, E, from sixth to first) so you're not constrained to alluding to them by number. A simple method to remember the open strings all together is to recollect the expression **Eddie Ate Dynamite; Good-Bye, Eddie.**

Frets: Fret can allude to either space where you put your left- hand finger or to the flimsy metal bar stumbling into the finger-board. At whatever point you manage guitar fingering, fret implies the space in the middle of the metal bars where you can serenely fit a left-hand finger The first fret is the locale between the nut (the slight, scored strip that isolates the headstock from the neck) and the principal metal bar. The fifth fret, at that point, is the fifth square up from the nut the locale between the 4th and 5th metal fret bars. A lot of guitars have a marker on the fifth fret, either an ornamental plan implanted in the fingerboard or a spot on the neck or both. One more purpose of business to settle up. You'll go over the terms open strings and worried strings starting here on in this book. This is what those terms mean:

- **Open string:** A string you play without pushing down on it with a left-hand finger.

- **Fretted string:** A string you play while pushing down on it at a specific fret.

Tuning Your Guitar with the fifth Fret Method

Relative tuning is so named because you don't have to bother with any outside reference to which you tune the instrument. For whatever length of time that the strings are in order in a specific relationship with one

12

another, you can make resonant and nice tones. Those equivalent tones may transform into sounds looking like those of a catfight if you attempt to cooperate with another instrument, be that as it may, yet as long as you tune the strings comparative with each other, the guitar is in line with itself. To tune a guitar by utilizing the relative technique, pick one string state, the sixth string as the beginning stage. Leave the pitch of that string with no guarantees; at that point, tune the various strings comparative with that sixth string. The fifth fret technique gets its name from the way that you quite often play a string at the fifth fret and then contrast the sound of that note with that of the following open string. You should be cautious, however, because the fourth fret (the fifth fret's envious understudy) places in an appearance close to the finish of the procedure.

Here's how to get your guitar in order by using the fifth fret strategy

1. Play the fifth fret of the sixth (low E) string (the fattest one, nearest to the roof) and then play the open fifth (A) string (the one close to it). Let the two notes ring together (as it were, let the sixth string to keep vibrating while you play the fifth string). Their pitches should coordinate precisely. If they don't appear to be very right, decide if the fifth string is lower or higher than the worried sixth string.

- If the fifth string appears lower, or flat, turn its tuning key with your left hand (in a counterclockwise bearing as you take a gander at the tuning key) to raise the pitch.

- If the fifth string appears to be sharp, or higher sounding, utilize its tuning key to bring down the pitch (by turning it a clockwise way as you take a gander at the tuning key). You may go

1

excessively far with the tuning key in case you're not cautious; provided that this is true, you have to invert your movements. On the off chance that you can't tell whether the fifth string is sequential, tune it flat deliberately (that is, tune it excessively low) and then return to the ideal pitch.

2. Play the fifth fret of the fifth (A) string and then play the open fourth. Here's how to get your guitar in order by utilizing the fifth fret technique (look at the chart in Figure 2-1 that plots every one of the five stages): Play the fifth fret of the sixth (low E) string (the fattest one, nearest to the roof) and then play the open fifth (A) string (the one close to it). Let the two notes ring together (as it were, permit the sixth string to keep vibrating while you play the fifth string). Their pitches should coordinate precisely. If they don't appear to be right, decide if the fifth string is lower or higher than the worried sixth string.

When the fifth string appears lower, or flat, turn its tuning key with your left hand (in a counterclockwise course as you take a gander at the tuning key) to raise the pitch. If the fifth string appears to be sharp or higher sounding, utilize its tuning key to bring down the pitch (by turning it a clockwise way as you take a gander at the tuning key). You may go excessively far with the tuning key in case you're not cautious; assuming this is the case, you have to switch your movements. On the off chance that you can't tell whether the fifth string is sequential, tune it flat purposefully (that is, tune it excessively low) and then return to the ideal pitch. Play the fifth fret of the fifth (A) string and then play the open fourth (D) string. Let both of these notes ring together. If the fourth string appears to be flat or sharp comparative with the worried fifth string, utilize the tuning key of the fourth string to change its pitch as needs are. Once more, in case you're uncertain about whether the fourth string is sequential, over tune it in one heading flat, or lower, is better and then return.

3. Play the fifth fret of the fourth (D) string and then play the open third (G) string. Let the two notes ring together once more. On the off chance that the third-string appears to be flat or sharp comparative with the worried fourth string, utilize the tuning key of the third-string to alter the pitch as needs are.

4. Play the 4th (and not the 5th!) fret of the third (G) string and then play the open second (B) string. Let the two strings ring together. If the second string appears to be flat or sharp, utilize its tuning key to change the pitch as needs are.

5. Play the fifth (truly, back to the fifth for this one) fret of the second (B) string and then play the open first (high E) string. Let the two notes ring together. If the first string appears to be flat or sharp, utilize its tuning key to alter the pitch likewise. In case you know that the two strings produce a similar pitch, you've currently tuned the upper (that is, upper as in more shrill) five strings of the guitar comparative with the fixed (untuned) sixth string. Your guitar's currently in line with itself. When you tune ordinarily, you utilize your left hand to turn the tuning peg. In any case, after you expel your finger from the string that you're worrying, it quits ringing; along these lines, you can no longer hear the string you're attempting to tune to (the worried string) as you change the open string. In any case, you can tune the open string while at the same time keeping your left-hand finger on the fret-ted string. Just utilize your correct hand! After you strike the two strings in progression (the worried string and the open string), take your correct hand and reach over your left hand (which remains fixed as you fret the string) and apply the tuning peg of the suitable string until the two strings sound precisely the equivalent.

Tuning Your Guitar to an External Source

Getting the guitar in line with itself through the fifth fret strategy in the former area is useful for your ear however isn't down to earth if you have to play with different instruments or voices that are familiar with standard tuning references.

"Experiencing the tuning fork," will be explained later in this part. If you need to carry your guitar with other instruments, you have to realize how to tune to a fixed source, for example, a piano, pitch pipe, tuning fork, or electronic tuner—utilizing such a source guarantees, that everybody is playing by similar tuning rules. Moreover, your guitar and strings are worked for ideal tone creation if you tune to standard pitch. The accompanying segments portray some common approaches to tune your guitar by utilizing fixed references. These strategies empower you to not just get in order yet, also make decent with the various instruments in the area.

Keying into the piano

Since it holds its pitch so well (requiring just semiannual or yearly tunings, contingent upon conditions), a piano is an incredible device to use for tuning a guitar. Expecting that you have an electronic keyboard or an all-around tuned piano around, you should simply coordinate the open strings of the guitar to the proper keys on the piano.

Giving that pitch pipe something to do

Clearly, in case you're headed toward the seashore with your guitar, you're not going to need to place a piano in the rear of your vehicle, regardless of whether you're extremely particular about tuning. So you need a little and increasingly commonsense gadget that provisions standard-tuning reference pitches. Enter the pitch pipe. The pitch pipe brings out pictures of harsh, ladylike theme pioneers. They press together their prune-like lips around a round harmonica to convey an iron-deficient squeak that in split-second marshals together the hesitant voices of the ensemble. However, pitch pipes fill their need. For guitarists, unique pitch pipes exist comprising of funnels that play just the notes of the open strings of the guitar (however sounding in a higher range) and none of them in the middle of notes. The upside of a pitch pipe is that you can hold it solidly in your mouth while playing, keeping your hands loose for tuning. The disadvantage of a pitch pipe is that you sometimes take some time to become acclimated to hearing a breeze produced pitch against a struck-string pitch. Be that as it may, with training, you can tune with a pitch pipe as effectively as possible with a piano. And a throw pipe tantrum significantly more effectively into your shirt pocket than a piano does!

Experiencing the tuning fork

After you get sufficient at recognizing pitches, you need just one single-pitched tuning reference to get your entire guitar in order. The tuning fork offers just one pitch, and it generally comes in just one flavor: A (the one above center C, which vibrates at 440 cycles for each second, generally known as A-440). In any case, that note's all you need. When you tune your open fifth string (A) to the tuning fork's A (although the guitar's A sounds in lower), you can tune each other string to that string by utilizing the relative tuning technique that we talk about in the area "Tuning Your Guitar to Itself with the fifth Fret Method" prior.

Applying a tuning fork

You should strike the fork against something firm, for example, a tabletop or kneecap, and then hold it near your ear or spot the stem (or handle) and not the tines (or fork prongs) against something that reverberates. This resonator can either be the tabletop again or the highest point of the guitar. (You can decide to hold it between your teeth, which makes your hands free! It really works, as well!) simultaneously, you should, in one way or another, play An and tune it to the fork's tone. The procedure is somewhat similar to pulling your house keys out of your pocket while you're stacked down with an armful of staple goods. The errand may not be simple, yet on the off chance that you do it enough, you, in the long run, become a specialist.

Choosing to use the electronic tuner

The fastest and most exact approach to get in order is to utilize an electronic tuner. This handy gadget appears to have black magic like forces. More up to date electronic tuners made particularly for guitars can generally detect what string you're playing, mention to you what pitch you're closest, and show whether you're flat (excessively low) or sharp (excessively high). About the main thing these gadgets don't do is turn the tuning keys for you (although we hear they're taking a shot at that). Some more established, diagram type tuners include a switch that chooses which string you need to tune.

CHAPTER 03

HOLDING AND READING GUITAR NOTATION

uitars are easy to use instruments. They fit nicely into the arms of
G most people, and how your two hands fall on the strings normally is
essentially the situation from which you should play. In this section, we
disclose to all of you about great stance procedures and how to hold your
hands similarly as though you were a youthful socialite at a completing
school. We quip since we give it a second thought. In any case, you truly
need to recollect that great stance and position, at any rate, forestall strain
and weariness and, best case scenario, help grow great focus propensities
and tone. After we get you situated effectively with the guitar, we go over
some essential music-translating abilities and tell you the best way to play
harmony.

Accepting the Positions

You may sit or stand while playing the guitar, and the position you pick
does not affect at all to your tone or procedure. A great many people want
to sit while rehearsing, however, stand while performing freely. (Note:
The one exemption to the sit or stand alternative is the old-style guitar,
which you ordinarily play in a sitting position. The conventional practice

is to play in a situated position as it were. This training doesn't imply that you can't play a traditional style guitar or old-style music whilestanding; however, the genuine quest for the old-style guitar necessitates that you sit while playing.

Sitting and playing a spell

Holding the guitar in a sitting position, rest the midsection of the guitar on your correct leg. (The midriff is the indented part between the guitar's upper and lower sessions, which are the distending bent parts that seem as though shoulders and hips.) Place your feet somewhat separated—equalization the guitar by gently resting your correct lower arm on the bass session. Try not to utilize the left hand to help the neck. You ought to have the option to take your left hand totally off the fretboard without the guitar plunging toward the floor. Old style guitar method, then again, expects you to hold the instrument to your left side leg, not to your right side. This position puts the focal point of the guitar closer to the focal point of your body, making the instrument simpler to play, particularly with the left hand, since you can more readily execute the troublesome fingerings of the traditional guitar music in that position. You should likewise hoist the old-style guitar, which you can do either by raising the left leg with an exceptionally made guitar footrest (the usual way) or by utilizing a helping arm, which moves between your left thigh and the guitar's lower side (the cutting-edge way). This gadget allows your left foot to stay on the floor and rather pushes the guitar open to question.

Standing up and performing.

To stand and play the guitar, you have to safely affix (or tie) a tie to both tie nails to the guitar. At that point, you can stand in a typical way and look at how cool you look in the mirror with that guitar threw over your shoulders. You may need to modify the lash to get the guitar at an open to playing height.

Fretting with your left hand

To get an idea of right left-hand situating on the guitar, broaden your left hand, palm up, and make a free clench hand, placing your thumb generally between your first and second fingers. All your knuckles ought to be twisted. Your hand should appear to be identical after you stick a guitar neck in there. The thumb coasts along the back of the neck, straighter than if you were making a clench hand but not unbending. The finger knuckles stay bowed maybe they're fretting or relaxed. Over, the left hand should fall in place naturally on the guitar neck as if you're getting a specially made tool that you've been utilizing all your life.

To fret a note, caress the tip of your finger down on a string, keeping your knuckles bowed. Attempt to get the fingertip to descend vertically on the string rather than at an angle. This position applies the greatest weight on the string and also keeps the sides of the finger from contacting adjacent strings which may cause either humming or quieting (deadening the string or keeping it from ringing). Utilize your thumb from its situation underneath the neck to help press the fingerboard for a more tightly hold.

When playing a special fret, remember that you don't place your finger straight on the metal fret wire but in the middle of the two frets (or between the nut and 1st fret wire). For instance, if you're playing the 5th fret, place your finger in the square between the fourth and fifth fret wires. Place it not in the focal point of the square (midway between the fret wires), but closer to the higher fret wire. This strategy gives you the clearest sound and forestalls humming.

Left-hand fretting requires quality, but don't be enticed to have a go at finding shortcuts towards fortifying your hands through artificial means. Working up the quality in your left hand takes time. You may see advertisements for hand-reinforcing gadgets and accept that these items may facilitate your left-hand endurance. Although we can't declare that these gadgets never work (and the same goes for the home-developed technique for crushing a racquet ball or tennis ball), one thing's without a doubt: Nothing causes you assemble your left-hand fretting quality preferred or faster over essentially playing guitar. Because of the quality your left hand applies while fretting, different parts of your body may worry to compensate. At intervals, ensure you relax your left shoulder, which has a propensity to ascend as you work on your fretting. Take visit "drop-shoulder" breaks. You may want to keep your upper arm and forearm parallel to the side of your body. Ease your elbow so it stays at your side. To maintain a decent left-hand position, you have to keep it comfortable and natural. If your hand starts to damage or ache, quit playing and take a rest. As with any other activity that requires muscular turn of events, resting enables your body to catch up. In the accompanying segments, we give you additional, specific details on left-hand fretting for electric and classical guitars.

Picking with your right hand

If you place a guitar in your lap and drape your correct arm over the upper session, your correct hand, held freely outstretched, crosses the strings at about a 60-degree angle. This position is useful for playing with a pick. For fingerstyle playing of guitar, you want to turn your correct hand increasingly perpendicular to the strings. For classical guitar, you may keep the correct hand as near a 90-degree angle as conceivable.

If you're utilizing a pick

You make all your electric guitar playing with a pick, regardless of whether you're belting out jammin, 'blues, jazz, nation, or pop. On acoustic guitar, you can play both with your fingers or with a pick. Both on electric and acoustic, you play most beat (harmony-based accompaniment) and virtually all lead (single-note tunes) by holding the pick, or plectrum (the good old term), between the thumb and forefinger.

If you're (playing beat), you hit the strings with the pick by utilizing wrist and elbow movement. The more vivacious the play, the more elbow you should place in with the general mish-mash. For playing lead, youutilize just the more economical wrist movement. Do not hold the pick too firmly as you play and plan on dropping it a lot for the initial barely any weeks that you use it. Picks come in many gauges. A pick's gauge shows how stiff, or thick, it is.

- Thinner picks are easier to manage for a starter. Medium picks are generally popular, because they're adaptable enough for comfortable beat playing yet stiff enough for leads.

- Heavy-gauge picks may appear to be cumbersome from the get go, but they're the decision for professionals, and eventually all skilled instrumentalists graduate to them (although a couple of famous holdouts exist Neil Young being a prime example).

If you're utilizing your fingers

If you shun such picks and want to go completely natural with your correct hand, you're fingerpicking (although you can finger-pick with special individual, wraparound picks that attach to your fingers called, confusingly enough, **fingerpicks**). Fingerpicking simply means you play the guitar by culling the strings with the persons right-hand fingers. The thumb usually plays the bass, or low, strings, and other fingers play the treble, or high, strings. In finger-picking, you utilize the tips of the fingers to play the strings, situating the hand over the sound gap (if you're playing acoustic) and keeping the wrist stationary but not inflexible. Maintaining a little arch in the wrist so the fingers descend all the more vertically on the strings also makes a difference.

Getting Your Head around Guitar Notation

Although you don't need to study music to play the guitar, musicians have built up a couple of straightforward deceives during that time that aid in communicating such basic ideas as song structure, harmony development, harmony movements, and important cadenced figures. Get on the shorthand gadgets for harmony diagrams, tablature, and beat slashes We guarantee that you don't have to study music to play the guitar. With the assistance of the harmony diagrams, tablature, and musicality slashes that we explain in this area, in addition to hearing what all this

22

stuff sounds like through the magic of audio tracks and video cuts, you can get on all that you have to understand and play the guitar.

Understanding harmony diagrams

Try not to stress reading a harmony diagram isn't care for reading music; it's far easier. All you have to do is understand where to put your fingers to shape a harmony. A harmony is characterized as the simultaneous sounding of at least three notes. The diagram quickly explains what the different parts of the diagram mean:

1. The network of six vertical lines and five horizontal ones speaks to the guitar fretboard, as if you place the guitar up on the floor or chair and took a look at the upper section of the neck from the front view.

2. The vertical lines speak to the guitar strings. The vertical line at the left is the low sixth string, and the right-most vertical line is the high first string.

3. The horizontal lines speak to frets. The thick parallel line at the top is the nut of the guitar, where the fretboard closes. So, the first fret is actually the subsequent vertical line from the top. (Try not to let the words here befuddle you; simply take a gander at the guitar.)

4. The spots that appear on vertical string lines between horizontal fret lines refer to notes that you fret.

5. The number straightforwardly beneath each string line (just underneath the last fret line) indicate which left-hand finger you

use to fret that note. On the left hand, 1 = pointer; 2 = center finger; 3 = ring finger; and 4 = little finger. You don't utilize the thumb to fret, with the exception of in certain unusual circumstances.

6. The X or O symbols above some string lines show strings that you leave open (unfretted) or that you don't play.

An O shows an open string that you do play.

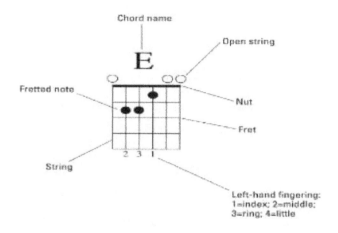

Image 2; A standard harmony diagram for an E harmony.

If a harmony starts on a fret other than the first fret, a numeral appears to one side of the diagram, close to the top fret line, to indicate in which fret you actually start. (In such cases, the top line isn't the nut.) In many cases, however, you deal primarily with chords that fall inside just the initial four frets of the guitar. Chords that fall inside the initial four frets typically utilize open strings, so they're alluded to as open chords.

Taking in tablature

Tablature (or only tab, for short) is a notation system that graphically speaks to the frets and strings of the guitar. Whereas harmony diagrams

32

do as such in a static way, tablature shows how you play music over some stretch of time. For all the musical examples that is shown in this book, you will see a tablature staff (or tab staff, for short) below the standard notation staff. This subsequent staff considers exactly what's going in the regular musical staff above it but in guitar language. Tab is guitar-specific in fact, many call it basically guitar tab. Tab doesn't mention to you what note to play, (for example, C or F or E). It does, however, mention to you what string to fret and where exactly on the fingerboard to fret that string.

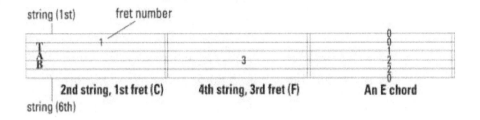

Image 3

Reading mood slashes

Musicians utilize a variety of shorthand stunts to indicate certain musical headings. They utilize this shorthand because, although a particular musical idea itself is normally simple enough, to notate that idea in standard composed music structure may demonstrate unduly complicated and cumbersome. So musicians utilize a map that gets the point across yet avoids the issue of reading (or composing) music. Mood slashes are slash marks (/) that basically reveal to you how to play rhythmically but not what to play. The harmony in your left hand figures out what you play.

Image 4

If you see such a harmony symbol with four slashes beneath it, as shown in the figure, you know to finger an E harmony and strike it multiple times. What you don't see, is a number of differently pitched notes sticking to various lines of a music staff, including several gap in-the-inside half notes and a large number of strong quarter notes so, any of that garbage that you expected to retain in high school just to perform "Mary Had a Little Lamb" . All you have to recollect on observing this particular diagram is to "play an E harmony multiple times." Simple, right?

Finding How to Play a Chord;

Chords are the basic structure squares of songs. You can play a harmony (the simultaneous sounding of at least three notes) several ways on the guitar by playing (dragging a pick or the back of your fingernails across the strings in a solitary, speedy movement), culling (with the individual right-hand fingers), or even slapping the strings with your free hand or clench hand. (Okay, that's rare, except if you're in a heavy metal band.) But you can't simply play any group of notes; you should play a group of notes arranged in some musically meaningful format.

For the guitarist, that implies learning any left-hand harmony structures. After you think you understand and understand the guitar notation we

32

portray in the previous segments, your most logical option is to hop directly in and play your first harmony. We propose that you start with E major, because it's a particularly guitar-accommodating harmony and one that you utilize a lot. After you get the hang of striking chords, you ultimately find that you can move many fingers into position simultaneously. For the time being, however, simply place your fingers each in turn on the frets and strings, as the accompanying guidelines indicate

- Place your first (forefinger) on the third string, first fret (actually between the nut and first fret wire but nearer to the fret wire). Try not to push down hard until you have your different fingers in place. Apply simply enough strain to shield your finger from getting off the string.

- Place your second (center) finger on the fifth string, second fret. Again, apply enough strain to keep your fingers in place. You currently have two fingers on the guitar, on the third and fifth strings, with an as-yet unfretted string (the fourth) in the middle.

- Place your third (ring) finger on the fourth string, second fret. There may be need to wriggle your ring finger a piece to get it to fit in there within the 1st and 2nd fingers and underneath the fret wire

Perhaps the hardest activity in playing chords is to avoid humming. Humming results if you're not pushing down very hard just when you fret. A hum can also result if a fretting finger accidentally interacts with an adjacent string, pre-venting that string from ringing uninhibitedly. Without expelling your fingers from the frets, have a go at "shaking and rolling" your fingers around on their tips to eliminate any hums when you play the harmony.

CHAPTER 04

THE BEST WAY TO BEGIN: STRUMMING CHORDS

F ollowing yourself as you sing your favorite songs or as someone else sings them is perhaps the most ideal ways to get basic guitar chords. If you can play basic chords, you can play many popular songs immediately from "Jump to My Lou" to "Louie." In this chapter, we organize the major and minor chords into families. A family of chords is essentially a group of related chords. We say they're related because you regularly utilize these chords together to play songs. The idea is similar to shading coordinating your clothing or assembling a group of food to create a balanced diet. Along the way, we assist you with expanding your guitar notation vocabulary as you start to build up your harmony playing and playing skills.

Think about a family of chords as a plant. If one of the chords the one that feels like command post in a song (usually the harmony you start and end a song with) is the plant's root, different chords in the family are the different shoots ascending from that same source. Collectively, the root and shoots make up the family. Put them collectively and you have a rich gardener, make that a song. Coincidentally, the technical term for a family is key. So you can say something like, "This song utilizes A-family chords" or "This song is in the key of A."

Chords in the A Family

The A family is a famous family for playing songs on the guitar because, as different families we present in this chapter, its chords are easy to play. That's because A-family chords contain open (strings that you play without pushing down any notes). Chords that embrace open strings are named open chords, or vacant position chords. Tune in to "Fire and Rain," by James Taylor, or "Tears in Heaven," by Eric Clapton, to hear the rhythm of a song that utilizes A-family chords. The basic chords in the A family include A, D, and E. Any of these chords is what's known as a major harmony. A harmony that's named by a letter name alone, for example, these (A, D, and E), is always major.

Fingering A-family chords

When playing chords, you utilize the "ball" of your fingertip, placing it simply behind the fret (as an afterthought toward the tuning pegs). Curve your fingers so the fingertips fall perpendicular to the neck. Ensure your left-hand fingernails are short so they don't keep you from squeezing the strings downward to the fingerboard.

Checking Chord Qualities

Chords have different qualities. You can characterize quality as the relationship between the different notes that make up the harmony — or essentially, what the harmony sounds like. Other than the quality of being major, other harmony qualities incorporate minor, seventh, minor

32

seventh, and major seventh. The accompanying rundown portrays each of these sorts of harmony qualities:

- Major chords: These are straightforward chords that have a stable sound.

- Minor chords: These are straightforward chords that have a delicate, sometimes sad sound.

- 7th chords: These are soul-filled, crazy sounding chords.

- Minor seventh chords: These chords sound smooth and jazzy.

- Major seventh chords: These chords sound brilliant and jazzy.

Each sort of harmony, or harmony quality, has a different sort of sound, and you can frequently recognize the harmony type just by hearing it. Tune in, for example, to the sound of a major harmony by playing A, D, and E. (For more information on seventh, minor seventh, and major seventh chords Try not to play any strings marked with a X (the sixth string on the A harmony and the fifth and sixth strings on the D harmony, for example). Strike only the main five (fifth through first) strings in the A harmony and the best four (fourth through first) strings in the D harmony. Specifically, striking strings may be awkward from the start, but keep at it and you'll get its hang. If you play a string marked with a X and we catch you, we'll renounce your picking privileges on the spot.

Playing A-family chords

Utilize your correct hand to play these A-family chords with one of the following:

1. A pick

2. Your thumb

3. The end of your nails (in a brushing movement toward the floor) Start playing from the most reduced pitched string of the harmony (the side of the harmony toward the roof as you hold the guitar) and play toward the floor.

Playing Callously

Playing chords can be somewhat painful from the get go. (We mean for you, not for individuals inside earshot; hey there, we're not that savage.) No matter how extreme you are, if you've never played the guitar, your left-hand fingertips are delicate. Fretting a guitar string, along these lines, is going to believe to your fingertips almost as if you're hammering a railroad spike with your bare hand. (Ouch!) to put it plainly, pushing down on the string harms. This situation isn't bizarre in any way in fact, it's very normal for starting guitarists. (Well, it's unusual if you appreciate the pain.)

You should create pleasant, thick calluses on your fingertips before playing the guitar can ever feel totally comfortable. It may take weeks or even a long time to develop those defensive layers of dead skin, contingent upon how much and how frequently you play. But after you eventually earn your calluses, you never lose them (totally, anyway). Like a Supreme Court equity, you're a guitar player forever. You can build up your calluses by playing the basic chords in this chapter again and again. As you progress, you also gain quality in your hands and fingers and become progressively comfortable in general when playing the guitar. Before you realise what's happening, fretting a guitar becomes as natural to you as shaking hands with your closest friend As with any physical-molding schedule, make sure you stop and rest if you start to feel delicacy or irritation in your fingers or hands. Working up those calluses takes time, and you can't cut time.

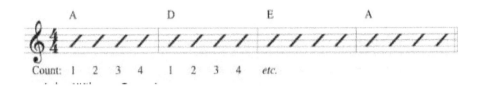

Image 5; A progression is essentially a progression of chords that you play consistently

A simple harmony movement in the key of An (utilizing just chords in the A family). After playing each harmony multiple times, you go to a vertical line in the music that follows the four play symbols. It's not something that you play. Bar lines naturally separate the music into smaller areas known as measures, or bars. (You can utilize these terms interchangeably; the two of them mean the same thing.) Measures make composed music easier to grasp, because they break up the music into little pieces.

Try not to hesitate or stop at the bar line. Keep your playing speed the same all through, even as you play "between the measures" that is, in the imaginary "space" from the finish of one measure to the start of the following that the bar line speaks to. Start out playing as gradually as necessary to assist you with keeping the beat steady. You can always accelerate as you get increasingly certain and capable in your harmony fingering and exchanging. By playing a movement again and again, you

4

start to grow left-hand quality and calluses on your fingertips. Attempt it (and attempt it and attempt it).

Chords in the D Family

The essential chords that make up the D family include D, Em (read: "E minor"), G, and A. The D family, hence, shares two basic open chords with the A family (D and An) and presents two new ones: Em and G. Because you already realize how to play D and A from the first segment, you have to work on just two additional chords (covered in the accompanying areas) to add the whole D family to your collection: Em and G. Tune in to "Here Comes the Sun," by the Beatles, or "Who Says," by John Mayer, to hear the sound of a song that utilizes D-family chords. Minor depicts the quality of a sort of harmony. A minor harmony has a sound that's unmistakably different from that of a major harmony. You may define the sound of a minor harmony as sad, distressed, scary, or even dismal. Note that the relationship of the notes that make up the harmony decides a harmony's quality. A harmony that's named by a capital letter followed by a small m is always minor.

Practicing and Improving

Saying that the more you practice, the better you'll get may sound obvious, but it's true. However, perhaps considerably progressively important is this idea: The more you practice, the faster you'll get great. Although there's no certain amount of rehearsal time for "getting great," a great standard is to practice at least 30 minutes consistently. Also, it's usually agreed that rehearsing at regular intervals is superior to jamming seven days of time (say, 3½ hours) all into one practice meeting. If from the start you locate another strategy difficult to master, stay with it, and you'll eventually get its hang. To improve on the guitar, we propose the accompanying:

- Set aside a certain time each day for rehearsing.

- Get together with your guitar-playing mates, and get them to tune in to what you're doing.

- Create a conducive rehearsing environment where you have privacy, away from distractions (TV, conversations, your mom pestering you to come to supper, and so on).

- Watch recordings of guitar players who play the sort of music you like and that you'd prefer to learn.

Attempt the following stunt to rapidly get how to play Em and to hear the difference between the major and minor harmony qualities: Play E, which is a major harmony, and then lift your forefinger off the third string. Presently you're playing Em, which is the minor-harmony adaptation of E. By rotating the two chords, you can simply hear the difference in quality among a major and minor harmony.

Notice the rotating fingering for G (2-3-4 rather of 1-2-3). As your hand gains quality and turns out to be increasingly adaptable, you want to change to the 2-3-4 fingering alternatively of the initially easier 1-2-3 fingering The additional symbol with the play symbol means that you play down toward the floor, and means that you play up toward the roof. (If you play your guitar while hanging in gravity boots, however, you should invert these last two directions.) The term "sim" is an abbreviation of the Italian word analogy, which teaches you to continue playing in a similar manner in this case, to continue playing in a down, down-up, down, down pattern.

If you're utilizing just your fingers for playing, play upstrokes with the back of your thumbnail at whatever point you see the symbol. Knowing the basic open chords in D family (D=Em=G= and An) allows you to play or practice a song in the key of D at this moment.

Chords in the G Family

By tackling related harmony families (as A, D, and G are), you carry over your insight from family to family as chords that you already know from previous families. The basic chords that comprises of the G family includes G, Am, C, D, and Em. If you already understand G, D, and Em (which we depict in the first areas on the An and D families), you can now attempt Am and C (canvassed in the accompanying segments). Tune in to "You've Got a Friend," as played by James Taylor, or "Each Rose Has Its Thorn," by Poison, to hear the sound of a song that utilizes G-family chords.

Playing G family chords

The new chords you have to play in the G family. Note that the playing of these two chords is alike: Each has finger 1 on the second string, first fret, and finger 2 on the fourth string, second fret. (Just finger 3 must change adding or expelling it in exchanging between these two chords.) In moving between these chords, keep these initial two fingers in place on the strings. Changing chords is always easier if you don't have to move all your fingers to new positions. The notes that different chords share is

42

known as normal tones. Notice the X over the sixth string in each of these chords. Try not to play that string while at the same time playing either C or Am.

Playing G-family chords

Play this movement again and again to get accustomed to exchanging chords and to develop those left-hand calluses. It gets easier after some time.

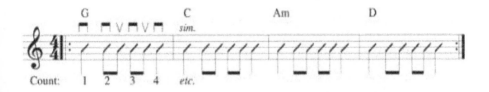

Image 6 A harmony movement you can play, utilizing just G-family chords.

Chords in the C Family

The last harmony family we have to examine is C. Some individuals say that C is the easiest key to play in. That's because C utilizes just the white-key notes of the piano in its musical scale and, as such, is kind of the music theory, one where everything (and, usually, everybody) starts in music. We decided to place the C family last in this chapter because it's anything but difficult to the point that it has lots of chords in its family beyond any reasonable amount to master all without delay.

The basic chords that comprises of the C family include C, Dm, Em, F, G, and Am. If you practice the previous areas on the A-, D-, and G-family chords, you know C, Em, G, and Am. (If not, look at them.) So, in this area, you have to get just two additional chords: Dm and F. After you know these two additional chords, you have all the basic major and minor chords we portray in this chapter under control. Tune in to "Residue in the Wind," by Kansas, or "Fortunate," by Jason Mraz and Colbie Caillat, to hear the sound of a song that utilizes C-family chords.

Fingering C-family chords

Notice that both the Dm and F chords have the second finger on the third string, second fret. Hold down this basic tone as you switch be-tween these two chords. Many people discover the F harmony the most difficult harmony to play of all the basic major and minor chords. That's because F utilizes no open strings, and it also requires a barre. A barre is what you're playing at whatever point you push down at least two strings on the double with a solitary left-hand finger. To play the F harmony, for example, you utilize your first finger to push down both the first and second strings at the first fret simultaneously.

You should apply extra finger strain to play a barre. You may find that, as you play the harmony (hitting the main four strings just, as the Xs in the harmony diagram indicate), you hear some hums or suppressed strings. Analysis with various placements of your pointer. Have a go at adjusting the angle of your finger or have a go at rotating your finger marginally on its side. Continue attempting until you discover a situation for the first finger that enables all four strings to ring clearly as you strike them.

Playing C-family chords

The Figure underneath shows a basic harmony movement you can play by utilizing C-family chords. Play the movement again and again to become accustomed to exchanging among the chords in this family and, obviously, to help develop those nasty little calluses. Video Clip 8 shows the right-hand movement for the syncopated figure in each bar.

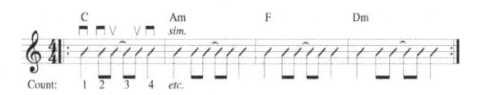

Image 7

Notice the small bended line joining the second half of beat 2 to beat 3. This line is known as a tie. A bind instructs you not to broadcast the second vibe of the two tied notes (in this case, the one on beat 3). Instead, simply continue holding the harmony on that beat (allowing it to ring) without restricting it with your correct hand.

The Basic Major and Minor Chords

As stated in the prologue to this chapter, you can play lots of popular songs immediately if you understand the basic major and minor chords. One important thing that you can do right currently is play oldies songs from the late '50s and early '60s, for example, "Earth Angel" and "Duke of Earl." These songs are centered on what's sometimes called the oldies movement. The oldies movement is a progression of four chords; they're repeated again and again to shape the accompaniment for a song.

You can play the oldies movement in any key, but the best guitar keys for the oldie's movement are C and G. In the key of C, the four chords that make up the movement are C=Am=F=G. And in the key G, the chords are G=Em=C=D. Take a stab at playing the movement in each key by playing four down-plays per harmony. Play the four chords again and again, in the succession given. If you need assistance with the fingerings for these chords, look at the areas "Chords in the C Family" and "Chords in the G Family," earlier in this chapter. The great starts as you sing oldies while accompanying yourself with the oldie's movement. As you sing a particular song, you locate that one of the keys (C or G) better suits your vocal range, so utilize that key. Playing oldies can become addicting, but fortunately, if you can't stop, you develop your calluses rapidly.

CHAPTER 05

MAKING THINGS SMOOTH BY PLAYING IN POSITION

One of the giveaways of starting guitar players is that they can play just down the neck, in vacant position. As you become acquainted with the guitar better, you discover you can utilize the entire neck to communicate your musical ideas. In this chapter, you adventure out of vacant position base camp into the higher altitudes of position playing.

Playing Scales and Practices in Position

As you tune in to complicated-sounding guitar music played by world class guitarists, you may think their left hands leaping around the fretboard with freedom. But usually, if you watch those guitarists in front of an audience or TV, you find that their left hands slightly move at all. Those guitarists are playing in position. Playing in position simply means that your left hand settles in a fixed location on the neck, with each finger pretty much on permanent assignment to a specific fret, and that you fret each note you don't utilize any open strings.

If you're playing in fifth situation, for instance, your 1st finger plays the 5th fret, your 2nd finger plays the 6th fret, your 3rd finger plays the 7th fret, and your 4th finger plays the 8th fret. A position, in this manner, gets its name from the fret that your first finger plays. (What guitarists call vacant position comprises of the combination of all the open strings in addition to the notes in first or second situation.)

In addition to allowing you to play notes anywhere they feel and sound best on the fingerboard (not exactly where you can most easily grab available notes, for example, the open-string notes in vacant position), playing in position makes you look cool like an expert! Consider it along these lines: A lay-up and a slam dunk are both worth two focuses in basketball, but just in the latter case does the announcer scream, "And the crowd goes wild!" In the accompanying segments, we explain the differences between playing in position and playing with open strings; we also give a lot of activities to assist you with getting comfortable with playing in position.

Playing in position as opposed to playing with open strings

Why play in position? Why not utilize vacant position and open strings all the time? We can give both of your key reasons:

- It's easier to play high-note tunes. Playing in vacant position allows you to play up to just the fourth or fifth fret. If you want to play higher tune than that, position playing allows you to play the notes easily and low-cost.

- You can immediately transpose any words or phrase that you know in position to another key basically by moving your hand to another position. Because position playing includes no open strings, all that you play in position is movable.

People have the knowledge that playing guitar in lower positions is comfortable than playing in higher ones. The higher notes really aren't harder to play; they're only harder to read in standard notation if you don't get excessively far in a conventional technique book (where reading high notes is usually saved for last). But here, you're concentrating on guitar playing rather than music reading so go for the high notes at whatever point you want.

Playing practices in position

The major scale (you know, which are do-re-me-fa-sol-la-ti-do tune you get by playing the white keys on the keyboard starting from key C) is a decent place to start practicing the skills you have to play in position. One important thing about playing in position is the placement of your left hand in particular, the position and setting of the fingers of your left hand. The following rundown contains tips for situating your left hand and fingers:

1. Set your fingers across the appropriate frets the whole time you're playing. Because you're in second situation for this scale, keep your first finger over the second fret, your second finger over the third fret, your third finger over the fourth fret, and your fourth finger over the fifth fret at all occasions regardless of whether they're not fretting any notes right now.

2. Keep all your fingers near the fretboard, ready to play. From the start, your fingers may display an inclination to straighten out and rise away from the fretboard. This propensity is natural, so work

to keep them twisted and to hold them down near the frets where they have a place for the position.

3. Relax! Although you may imagine that you have to strongly center all your vitality on playing out this move effectively or situating that finger to make sure you don't. What you're progressing in the direction of is necessarily embracing the most characteristic and loosened up way to deal with playing the guitar. (You may not think it's normal now, yet in the long run, you'll get the idea. Seriously!) To make things simple, yet stay mindful of your developments. Is your left shoulder, for instance, riding up like Quasimodo's? Check it occasionally to ensure it remains strain-free. What's more, make certain to take visit full breaths, particularly on the off chance that you feel yourself taking care of.

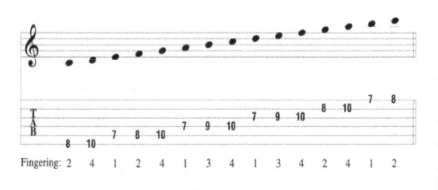

Image 8

To assist you with making sure to hold your fingers over the proper frets constantly (regardless of whether they're not playing right now) and keep your fingers near the fretboard; we have a turn on an old articulation: Keep your companions close, your enemies closer, and your frets significantly closer. Work on playing the scale appeared in Figure above all over the neck, utilizing exchange picking. If you remember the fingering design (appeared under the tab numbers), you can play any significant scale sim-handle by moving your hand up or down to an alternate position. Attempt it. And afterward challenge the closest piano player to a transposing (key-evolving) challenge, utilizing a significant scale.

Moving positions

Music isn't easy to such an extent that you can play it across the board position, and life would be truly static if you could. In certifiable circumstances, you should frequently play a continuous section that takes you through various positions. To do so effectively, you have to ace the position move with the assurance of an old lawmaker.

Making your activities to assemble quality and expertise

A few people do a wide range of activities to build up their position playing. They purchase books that contain only position-playing works out. A portion of these books expect to create sight-understanding aptitudes, and others plan to grow left-hand finger quality and skill. However, you don't generally need such books. You can make up your activities to construct finger quality and finesse. (Also, sight perusing doesn't concern you now at any rate, since you're perusing tab numbers.)

To make your activities, simply take the two-octave significant scale demonstrated before in Figure above and number the 15 notes the scale as 1 through 15. At that point, make up a couple of basic scientific blends that you can work on playing. Following are a few models:

- 1-2-3-1, 2-3-4-2, 3-4-5-3, 4-5-6-4, etc. See figure a, image 9
- 1-3-2-4, 3-5-4-6, 5-7-6-8, 7-9-8-10, etc. See figure b, image 9
- 15-14-13, 14-13-12, 13-12-11, 12-11-10, thus on. See figure c, image 9

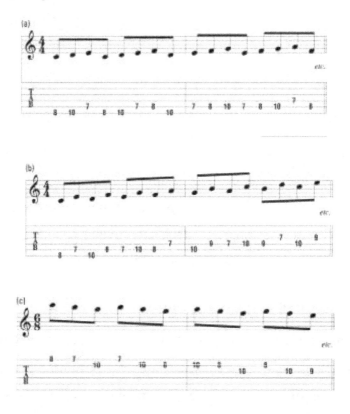

Image 9

Three instances of examples to help develop the left hand. Figure a,b,c shows how these numbers look in music and tab. Keep in mind; these notes are simply recommended examples to retain and help produce mastery. You get the idea. You can make up several stages and practice them forever or until you get exhausted. Piano understudies have a book called Hanon that contains loads of scale stages to help create quality and freedom of the fingers. You can look at that book for change thoughts; however, making up your own is similarly as simple.

Rehearsing Songs in Position

Certain keys fall nicely into specific situations on the guitar. Melodies are situated in keys, so if you play a tune in a specific key, the tune will likewise fall serenely into a specific position. Rock, jazz, blues, and nation lead was playing all certain interest situations to render a bona fide sound. Revealing to you that the tune of a melody sounds best on the off chance that you play it in one position as opposed to another may appear to be somewhat subjective to you. In any case, trust us on this one, that playing a "Chuck Berry lick in An" is practically unimaginable in anything other than the fifth position. Nation licks that you play in A, then again, fall most serenely in the second position, and attempting to play them anyplace else is simply making things hard on yourself.

Note: That's another incredible aspect with the guitar: The best situation for a specific style sounds best to your ears, yet additionally feels best to your hands. Also, that is the thing that makes playing the guitar so much fun. Play these tunes by perusing the tab numbers and tuning in to the soundtracks; notice how cool exciting the neck feels as opposed to making light of path in a vacant position, where those fledglings play. At whatever point you're playing in position, make certain to keep your left submit a fixed position, opposite to the neck, with your first finger at a given fret and different fingers following all together, one for each fret. Hold the fingers over the suitable frets near the fretboard, regardless of whether they're not worrying notes right now.

CHAPTER 06

DOUBLING UP WITH DOUBLE-STOPS

A twofold stop is guitar language for playing two notes simultaneously something the guitar can do without hardly lifting a finger yet that is outlandish on woodwinds and just insignificantly fruitful on bowed string instruments. (As a matter of fact, guitarists lifted the term from violin playing, however immediately made twofold stops their own.) This section gives you the scoop on the best way to play twofold stops. Incidentally, you don't do anything extraordinary in worrying twofold stops. Fret them a similar way you would harmonies or single notes.

Starting with the Basics of Double-Stops

You experience the guitar's capacity to play more than one note at the same time as you play a harmony; however, you can likewise play more than one note in a melodic setting. Playing twofold stops is an incredible method to play incongruity with yourself. So proficient in the guitar at playing twofold stops, truth be told, that some melodic structures, for example, '50s awesome, 'nation, and Mariachi music (you know, the music that Mexican road groups play) utilize twofold stops as a sign of their styles. In the accompanying areas, we characterize twofold stops and assist you with getting settled with them by giving a couple of activities.

Characterizing twofold stops

A twofold stop is just two notes that you play at the same time. It falls somewhere close to a solitary note (one note) and a harmony (at least three notes). You can play a twofold stop on nearby strings or on nonadjacent strings (by skipping strings). The models and tunes that you find in this part, in any case, include just neighboring twofold string stops, since they're the simplest to play. If you play a song in twofold stops, it sounds better and more extravagant, fuller and more resonant than if you play it by utilizing just single notes. What's more, if you play a riff in twofold stops, it sounds gutsier and fuller the twofold stops simply make a greater sound. Look at some Chuck Berry riffs "Johnny B. Goode," for instance and you can hear that he utilizes twofold stops constantly.

Attempt to practices in twofold stops

You can play twofold stops in two general manners: by utilizing just one set of strings (the initial two strings, for instance) moving the twofold plugs here and there the neck or in one territory of the neck by utilizing distinctive string sets and moving the twofold stops over the neck (first playing the fifth and fourth strings, for instance, and afterward the fourth and third, etc.).

Playing twofold plugs all over the neck

Start with a C-significant scale that you play in twofold stop 3rds (takes note of that are two-letter names separated, for example, C-E, D-F, and so on), solely on the initial two strings, climbing the neck. This sort of twofold stop design shows up in Figure 8-1. The left-hand fingering doesn't show up underneath the tab numbers in this score, yet that is not hard to make sense of. Start with your first finger for the main twofold stop. (You need just one finger to worry this first twofold stop because the first string is open.) Then, for the various dual stops in the scale, use fingers 1 and 3 if the notes are two frets separated (the second and third twofold stops, for instance) and use 1st and 2nd fingers if the notes are one fret separated (the fourth and fifth twofold stops, for instance). With your correct hand, strike just the first and second strings. View Video Clip 31 to see the rising movement of the left hand and the right fingerings.

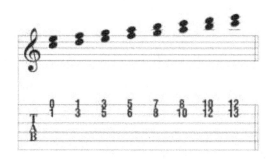

Image 10

A C-significant scale that you play in twofold quits, climbing the neck on one set of strings.

Playing twofold stops over the neck.

Playing twofold stops over the neck is likely more often than playing the neck here and there on a string pair. a C-significant scale that you play in 3rds in a vacant position, moving over the neck; Once more, the model doesn't show the fingerings for each twofold stop; however you can utilize the 1st and 2nd finger if the notes are one fret separated (the main twofold stop, for instance) and fingers 1 and 3 if the notes are two frets separated (the subsequent twofold stop, for instance).

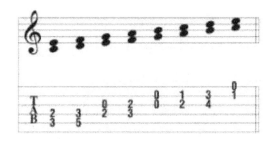

Image 11

A C-significant scale that you play in twofold quits, moving over the neck in an empty position. What's particularly basic in rock and blues tunes is playing twofold stops over the neck where the two notes that make up the twofold stop are on a similar fret (which you play as a two-string barre).

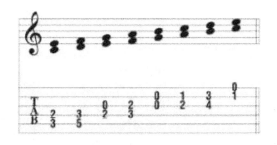

Image 12

To hear twofold stops in real life, tune in to the opening of Jimmy Buffett's "Margaritaville," Leo Kottke's variant of the Allman Brothers' "Little Martha," Van Morrison's "Earthy colored Eyed Girl," Chuck Berry's "Johnny B. Goode," the introductions to Simon and Garfunkel's "Toward home Bound" and "Bookends," and the introduction to Jason Mraz's "I Won't Give Up.

Playing Songs in Double-Stops

Double-stops can make your playing sound cool (as when Chuck Berry shakes out on "Johnny B. Goode"), or they can make your melodic entries sound additional sweet (as when two vocalists orchestrate with one another). In the songs that follow, you get the chance to sound both cool ("Double-Stop Rock") and sweet ("Aura Lee" and "The Streets of Laredo"). So, prepare your fingers to shape lots of minimal two-note chords (twofold stops, that is) on these treats. As we said, to keep things overall quite easy, we place all the twofold stops on adjacent strings (no quieting of "in the middle of" strings necessary!). And here's a tip to make things especially easy: When the two notes of a twofold stop fall on the same fret (which happens a lot in the Chuck Berry–motivated "Twofold Stop Rock"), play them as a small barre (with a solitary finger). Here's some valuable information to assist you in playing the songs:

•**Aura Lee: To play this song** made famous by Elvis Presley as "Love Me Tender" you have to realize how to play twofold plugs all over the neck on the first and second string. In the twofold stop scales that you practice in above, the two notes of the twofold plug go up or down altogether. In "Aura Lee," both notes of the twofold stop sometimes move in the same bearing and sometimes in inverse ways. On different occasions, one of the notes goes up or down while the difference remains stationary. Blending headings makes an arrangement all the more intriguing. Play and tune in to "Aura Lee," and you understand. Then note that the left-hand fingerings appear below the tab numbers. If the same finger plays perfect notes, but at different frets, a slanted line indicates the position shift. For your right-hand picking, utilize all downstrokes.

Make sure to repeat the initial four bars (as the repeat signs around them indicate) before proceeding to bar 5.

CHAPTER 07

STRETCHING OUT: BARRE CHORDS

This section will explain how to play chords that you can move all around the neck. Not at all like vacant position chords, which can be played distinctly in one place, movable chords can be played at any fret. In the greater part of these movable chords, you play what's called a barre (articulated "bar"). When you play a barre, one of your left-hand fingertips (normally the list) pushes down all or a large portion of the strings at a certain fret, enabling the remaining fingers to play a harmony structure immediately above (toward the body of the guitar) the barre finger. Think about your barre finger as a kind of movable nut or capo and your remaining fingers as playing certain vacant position harmony shapes legitimately above it.

A movable barre harmony contains no open strings just fretted notes.

You can move these fretted notes up or below the neck to different situations to produce different chords of the same quality. Adjustable barre chords can either be E-based, getting their names from the notes you play on the sixth (low E) string or A-based, getting their names from the notes you play on the fifth (A) string. We spread both of these kinds of chords in this chapter. We also give you a brisk exercise on power chords, which are chords that are neither major nor minor and are usually made up of simply the most minimal a few strings of a barre harmony or vacant position harmony. Major Barre Chords Focused on E One of the most helpful movable barre chords is the one based on the open E harmony.

Starting with a open- position E harmony

An ideal way to get it together on major barre chords based on E is to start with a vacant position E harmony. Follow these methods

1. Play an open E harmony, but instead of utilizing the normal 2-3-1 remaining hand fingering, use fingers 3-4-2. This fingering leaves your first (forefinger) free, floating above the strings.

2. Set your first finger down over all six strings on the oppositeside of the nut (the side toward the tuning pegs). Setting your pointer across the strings at this location doesn't affect the sound of the harmony because the strings do not sound on that side of the nut. Expanding your first finger across the width of the strings, however, causes you to get the "vibe" of a barre harmony position. Try not to press excessively hard with any of your fingers, because you're going to move the harmony.

3. Take the whole left-hand shape from Step 2 and slide it up (toward the body of the guitar) one fret, so your first finger is barring the first fret, and your E-harmony fingers have all moved up a fret as well. You're currently in an F-harmony position (because F is one fret higher than E), and you can push down across all the strings with your forefinger.

4. Try playing the notes of the harmony each string in turn (from the sixth string to the first) to see whether all the notes ring out clearly. The initial few occasions you attempt this harmony, the chances are acceptable that some of the notes won't ring clearly and that your left-hand fingers are going to hurt.

You can utilize this "sliding up from a vacant position harmony" method to frame all the barre chords in this chapter. (But we also furnish you with another approach in later segments.) Having challenges at first in creating a barre F is normal (challenging maybe, but normal). So, before you abandon the guitar and take up the sousaphone, here are some tips to assist you with nailing this vexing harmony:

- Make sure you line up your left-hand thumb at the back of the guitar neck under the point between your 1st and 2nd fingers. This position gives you maximum leverage while applying pressure.

- Instead of holding your 1st finger completely flat, switch it a little onto its side.

- Progress the elbow of your left arm in near your body, even to the point that it's contacting your body at the waist. As you play vacant position chords, you find that you usually hold your elbow marginally away from your body. Not so with full barre chords.

- If you hear stifled strings, verify that your left-hand fingers are contacting just the appropriate strings and not keeping adjacent ones from ringing. Have a go at applying more weight with the fingers and make sure to play on the very tips for extra clearance. Calluses and experience assist you with getting a clear sound from

6

a barre harmony. You have to apply more strain to fret at the base of the neck (at the 1st fret) than you do at, say, the 5th fret. Have a go at moving your F harmony here and there the neck to different frets on the guitar to demonstrate to yourself that playing the harmony gets easier as you climb the neck. Remember that the quintessence of this harmony structure is that it's movable. Not at all like what your elementary teachers may have let you know, don't sit so still! Move around already! Playing or rehearsing barre chords on an electric guitar is very easy than playing them on an acoustic guitar. If you're utilizing an acoustic and you're having an issue with barre chords, give playing them a shot an electric (but not one of those el-cheapo ones from the pawnshop) and take note of the difference. Doing so may move you to keep at it.

Finding the correct fret for each major E-based barre harmony

Because you can play an F harmony as a barre harmony, you can now, through the miracle of movable chords, play each major harmony all 12 of them just by climbing the neck. To decide the name of each harmony, you have to comprehend what note name you're playing on the sixth (low E) string because all E-based barre chords get their name from the sixth string (similarly as the open E harmony does). Each fret is a half advance away from each adjacent fret. So if a first fret barre harmony is F, the second fret barre harmony is F; the third fret harmony is G; the fourth fret is G; and so on. After you reach the 12th fret, the notes and in this way, the barre harmonies that you play at those frets repeat: The thirteenth fret barre harmony is the same as the first (F); the 14th is the same as the 2nd

(F); and so on. The frets work similarly to a clock: 13 equals 1, 14 equals 2, and so on.

Playing movements utilizing major barre chords based on E

A decent way to manufacture your solace and trust in playing barre chords is by practicing a movement, which is a progression of chords. Utilize just barre chords for this activity (and for all the activities in this chapter), regardless of whether you realize how to play these chords as vacant position chords. Play the C harmony, for example, by barring at the eighth fret. At that point, play An at the fifth fret, G at the third fret, and F at the first fret. Utilize the F-harmony fingering for all these chords.

Attempting to make all six strings ring out clearly on each harmony can get a bit tiring. You can give your left-hand fingers some ease by releasing weight as you slide, starting with one harmony then onto the next. This action of flexing and releasing can assist you with building up a little artfulness and shield you from tiring so easily. You don't have to keep a "Vulcan Death Grip" on the neck all the time — just while you're playing the harmony. Although you can stop everything if your hand starts to cramp, attempt to keep at it; as with any physical endeavor, you eventually develop your quality and stamina.

Truthfully, barre chords are the triathlon of guitar playing, so strap on your best Ironman regalia and feel the consume. To demonstrate the versatility of barre-harmony movements, here's an example that has a syncopated play and sounds similar to the music of the Kinks. In syncopation, you either inspire an emotional response (or note) where you

6

don't hope to hear it or fail to hit home (or note) where you do hope to hear it.

Minor, Dominant seventh, and Minor seventh Barre Chords Based on E

After you're familiar with the basic feel and development of the major barre chords portrayed earlier in this chapter, start adding other harmony qualities into your collection (which is a fancy French word for "bag of stunts" that musicians often use in talking about their music). Fortunately, all that you think about moving chords around the neck area to get a clear, ringing tone out of the personal notes in harmony (you are practicing, aren't you?) and the flex-and-release action that you use in playing major barre chords — carries over to different types of barre chords. Playing a minor, a dominant seventh, or a minor seventh barre structure is no more physically challenging than playing a major barre. Hence, as you practice all the various barre chords in the accompanying areas, you should start to see things getting somewhat easier.

Mastering minor chords

Framing an E-based minor barre harmony is similar to shaping a major barre harmony, which we explain in the means in the segment "Starting with a vacant position E harmony. You can follow that arrangement of steps, starting with an open Em harmony but fingering it with fingers 3 and 4 (instead of how you usually finger the harmony, Next, lay your 1st finger across the strings on the opposite side of the nut and then slide the shape up one fret, creating an Fm harmony. As we stated earlier in this chapter, you can utilize this "sliding up from a vacant position harmony"

SURFHGXUH WR IUDPH DOO WKH EDUUH FKRUGV LQ WKLV FKDSWHU. %XW \RX GRQ'W KDYH WR H[SHULHQFH DOO WKDW.

7KH IROORZLQJ EDVLF DGYDQFHV GHSLFW DQRWKHU ZD\ WR DSSURDFK WKH)P EDUUH KDUPRQ\:

F

134211

,PDJH 13

3OD\ DQ) PDMRU EDUUH KDUPRQ\. 6HH WKH DUHD "6WDUWLQJ ZLWK D YDFDQW SRVLWLRQ (KDUPRQ\," HDUOLHU LQ WKLV FKDSWHU.

Fm

134111

,PDJH 14

7DNH DZD\ \RXU VHFRQG ILQJHU IURP WKH WKLUG VWULQJ. 7KH ILUVW ILQJHU EDUUH, ZKLFK LV DOUHDG\ SXVKLQJ GRZQ DOO WKH VWULQJV, QRZ IUHWV WKH QHZ QRWH RQ WKH WKLUG VWULQJ. 7KDW'V DOO \RX KDYH WR GR. <RX LQVWDQWO\ FKDQJH D PDMRU EDUUH KDUPRQ\ WR D PLQRU EDUUH KDUPRQ\ E\ H[SHOOLQJ RQO\ RQH ILQJHU. 7R SOD\DQ $P EDUUH KDUPRQ\, IRU H[DPSOH, \RX VLPSO\PRYH WKH EDUUH WR WKH ILIWK IUHW.

,I \RX'UH XQFHUWDLQ DERXW ZKHWKHU \RX'UH SOD\LQJ D EDUUH KDUPRQ\ DW WKH ULJKW IUHW, KDYH D JR DW DOWHUQDWLQJ WKH KDUPRQ\ ZLWK LWV YDFDQW SRVLWLRQ structure, playing first the barre, and then the open structure. Play the two forms in rapid succession multiple times. You can then hear if the two chords are exact or different. Have a go at playing the basic movement shown in Figure BELOW, which utilizes both major and minor barre chords (play C at the eighth fret, Am at the fifth fret, Fm at the first fret, and G at the third fret).

Image 15

Utilizing both major and minor barre chords in a movement. The dabs above the slashes in bars 2 and 4 of figure above are **called staccato marks**. They advise you to stop the notes. (Instead of playing daahh-daahh-daahh, play di-di-di.) The ideal way to slice these notes short is to release your left-hand finger pressure somewhat directly after you play the harmony. The symbols at the finish of the measures 2 and 4 are called rests. Try not to play during a rest. Presently take a stab at playing the higher than the Figure indicates. This two-fret variation gives you a D-Bm-Gm-A movement. You've quite recently transposed (changed the key of) the movement rapidly and easily through the magic of movable chords! Diving into dominant seventh chords, Dominant seventh chords have a sharper, more perplexing sound than do straight major chords. Changing to a barre dominant seventh harmony from a major barre harmony, however, is similarly as easy as changing from a major to a minor barre harmony you simply lift a solitary (although different) finger.

7R FKDQJH DQ) PDMRU EDUUH KDUPRQ\ LQWR DQ)7 EDUUH KDUPRQ\, IROORZ WKHVH PHDQV:

F

134211

,PDJH 16

)LQJHU DQ) PDMRU EDUUH KDUPRQ\, DV ZH GHSLFW LQ WKH DUHD "6WDUWLQJ ZLWK D YDFDQW SRVLWLRQ(KDUPRQ\,"HDUOLHU LQ WKLV FKDSWHU.

F7

131211

,PDJH 17

([SHO\RXU IRXUWK ILQJHU IURP WKH IRXUWK VWULQJ. 7KH ILUVW ILQJHU EDUUH QRZ IUHWV WKH KDUPRQ\'V QHZ QRWH. 7DNH D VWDE DW SOD\LQJ WKH EDVLF PRYHPHQW VKRZQ XQGHUQHDWK, XWLOL]LQJ PDMRU DQG GRPLQDQW VHYHQWK EDUUH FKRUGV (SOD\ * DW WKH WKLUG IUHW, $7 DW WKH ILIWK IUHW, & DW WKH HLJKWK IUHW, DQG ▾7 DW WKH WHQWK IUHW).

,PDJH 18 XWLOL]LQJ PDMRU DQG GRPLQDQW VHYHQWK EDUUH FKRUGV LQ D PRYHPHQW.

3OD\LQJ WKH PRYHPHQW LQ)LJXUH DERYH LQ GLIIHUHQW NH\V LV DV VWUDLJKWIRUZDUG DV VWDUWLQJ LQ D ORFDWLRQ GLIIHUHQW IURP WKH WKLUG IUHW DQG PRYLQJ WKH VDPH UHODWLYH GLVWDQFH.)URP DQ\ SODFH \RX VWDUW, VXEVWDQWLDOO\ FOLPE WZR IUHWV IRU WKH VXEVHTXHQW KDUPRQ\, XS WR WKUHH DGGLWLRQDO IUHWV IRU WKH WKLUG KDUPRQ\, DQG WKHQ XS WZR DGGLWLRQDO IUHWV IRU WKH IRXUWK KDUPRQ\. 3URQRXQFH WKH QDPHV RI WKH FKRUGV \RX SOD\ VR DQ\RQH FDQ KHDU WR VXSSRUW \RX FRQQHFW WKHLU QDPHV ZLWK WKHLU ORFDWLRQV. $OWKRXJK DGMXVWDEOH FKRUGV PDNH WUDQVSRVLQJ RQ WKH JXLWDU HDV\, UHPHPEHULQJ RQO\ WKH SDWWHUQ RI WKH KDQG GHYHORSPHQW LQVWHDG RI WKH DFWXDO KDUPRQ\ QDPHV \RX'UH SOD\LQJ LV IDU HDVLHU. $IWHU HQRXJK RFFDVLRQV WKURXJK, \RX QDWXUDOO\ FRPH WR UHDOL]H WKDW \RX SOD\, IRU H[DPSOH, D %7 KDUPRQ\ DW WKH VHYHQWK IUHW.

7U\LQJ PLQRU VHYHQWK FKRUGV

0LQRU VHYHQWK FKRUGV KDYH D PLOGHU, MD]]LHU, DQG PRUH XQSUHGLFWDEOH VRXQG WKDQ VWUDLJKW PLQRU FKRUGV GR. <RX FDQ VKDSH D PLQRU VHYHQWK (-EDVHG EDUUH KDUPRQ\ E\ EDVLFDOO\ MRLQLQJ WKH DFWLRQV \RX GHWHUPLQH WR FKDQJH WKH PDMRU VFDOH WR PLQRU DQG PDMRU WR GRPLQDQW VHYHQWK. 7R FKDQJH DQ) PDMRU EDUUH KDUPRQ\ LQWR DQ)P7 EDUUH KDUPRQ\, IROORZ WKHVH PHDQV:

,PDJH 19

3OD\ DQ) PDMRU EDUUH KDUPRQ\, DV ZH GHSLFW LQ WKH VHJPHQW "6WDUWLQJ
ZLWK D YDFDQW SRVLWLRQ (KDUPRQ\,)"HDUOLHU LQ WKLV FKDSWHU.

Fm7

131111

,PDJH 20

5HPRYH \RXU VHFRQG ILQJHU IURP WKH WKLUG VWULQJ DQG \RXU IRXUWK ILQJHU
IURP WKH IRXUWK VWULQJ. 7KH ILUVW ILQJHU EDUUH, ZKLFK LV DOUHDG\ SXVKLQJ
GRZQ DOO WKH VWULQJV, IUHWV WKH QHZ QRWHV RQ WKH WKLUG DQG IRXUWK VWULQJV.

**OLQRU, 'RPLQDQW VHYHQWK, OLQRU VHYHQWK, DQG ODMRU VHYHQWK %DUUH
&KRUGV %DVHG RQ $**

:H DGPLW WKDW WKH $-EDVHG PDMRU EDUUH KDUPRQ\ LV VRPHWKLQJ RI DQ
RGGEDOO DV IRU OHIW-KDQG ILQJHULQJ. %XW DOO WKH RWKHU $-EDVHG VWUXFWXUHV DUH
VXEVWDQWLDOO\ PRUH ORJLFDO DQG FRPIRUWDEOH DV IDU DV OHIW-KDQG ILQJHULQJ.
)RU WKH UHPDLQGHU RI WKH $-EDVHG VWUXFWXUHV LQ WKH DFFRPSDQ\LQJ DUHDV,
\RX GRQ'W H[SHULHQFH DQ\ SHFXOLDU KDQG EHQGLQJ RU QHZ VWUDWHJLHV. $OO \RX
GR LV JHW D YDULHW\ RI GLIIHUHQW VWUXFWXUHV WR LPSURYH \RXU KDUPRQ\
YRFDEXODU\.

OLQRU FKRUGV 7R IUDPH DQ $-EDVHG PLQRU EDUUH KDUPRQ\, \RX FRXOG
IROORZ VWHSV VLPLODU WR WKH RQHV WKDW ZH SRUWUD\ LQ WKH VHJPHQW ")LQJHULQJ
WKH $-EDVHG PDMRU EDUUH KDUPRQ\,"HDUOLHU LQ WKLV FKDSWHU: 3OD\ DQ RSHQ
$P KDUPRQ\ E\ XWLOLJLQJ D 3-4-2 ILQJHULQJ LQVWHDG RI 2-3-1 LI \RX QHHG
DVVLVWDQFH ZLWK WKH RSHQ $P KDUPRQ\); OD\ \RXU ILUVW ILQJHU GRZQ DFURVV

all the strings on the opposite side of the nut; and then slide the shape up one fret and press down solidly, delivering a Bfm harmony.

Power Chords

A power harmony is usually just the most reduced a few notes of a regular vacant position or barre harmony. Guitarists regularly use power chords in awesome music to create a flat sound. Power chords are very easy to play than are their full-variant counterparts and don't include a major or minor quality to them; therefore, they can stand in for either sort of harmony. Additionally, as you discover in the accompanying areas, they're very amusing to play!

Fingering power chords

A power harmony comprises of just two different notes that are always five stages apart, for example, An E or C-G. (Tally letter names on your fingers to affirm that A to E and C to G are five stages apart.) But the actual harmony that you play may include multiple strings, because you may be multiplying either of the notes that make up the power harmony that is, playing the same notes in several octaves (and on separate strings). As do most different chords, power chords come in two varieties:

Open-position: We show you the most widely recognized vacant position power chords — E5, A5, and D5 These chords are just a few least notes of the basic vacant position E, An, and D chords.

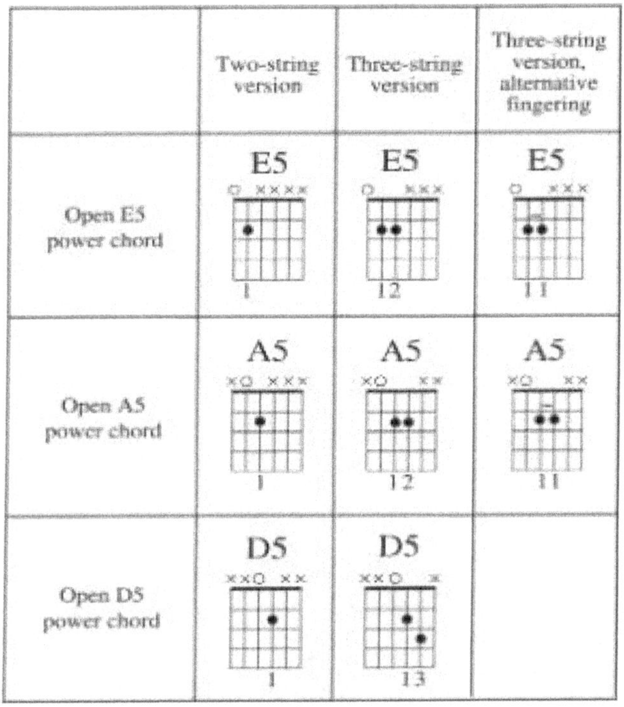

	Two-string version	Three-string version	Three-string version, alternative fingering
Open E5 power chord	E5	E5	E5
Open A5 power chord	A5	A5	A5
Open D5 power chord	D5	D5	

Image 21

Movable: Movable power chords are just a few most reduced notes of the movable barre chords that we depict earlier in this chapter. As is the case with adjustable barre chords, adjustable power chords can either be E-based, getting their names right from the notes you play on the sixth (low E) string or A-based, getting their names from the notes you play on the fifth (A) string. Remember that power chords are well fit to a heavier, mutilated sound, and you can utilize them in place of full forms of chords because they usually contain the same base a few notes. So, if you're feeling somewhat defiant, somehow devilish, pick up your guitar and play "We Wish You a Merry Christmas," including power chords, a misshaped sound, and a really bad attitude.

We Wish You a Merry Christmas

Image 22

CHAPTER 08

MAKING THE GUITAR TALK

rticulation alludes to how you play and interface notes on the guitar. Look at it along these lines: If pitches and rhythms are what you play, articulation is how you play. Articulation gives your music articulation and enables you to make your guitar talk, sing, and even cry.

From a technical standpoint, such articulation methods as hammer-ons, pull-offs, slides, and curves enable you to associate notes together easily, giving your playing a bit "grease." Vibratos add life to support (or held) notes that, in any case, simply stay there like a dead turtle, and quieting shapes the sound of individual notes, giving them a tight, cut sound. As you start to include articulation in your playing, you start to practice more authority over your guitar. You're not just playing "accurately" you're playing with someone's style. This chapter reveals how to play all the articulation strategies you have to get your guitar talking. After we explain each method, we present some idiomatic licks (musical phrases that naturally suit a particular procedure or style), so you can play the strategy in con-content.

Hitting Hammer-Ons

A hammer-on doesn't allude to playing the guitar while wearing a tool belt; a hammer-on is a left-hand strategy that enables you to play two continuous ascending notes by picking just the main note. The hammer-on gets its name from the movement of your left-hand finger, which appears like a hammer striking the fretboard, making a note of that fret to sound. This method, which we depict in detail in the accompanying areas, makes the association between the notes sound smooth far more rhythmic than if you necessarily pick each note separately. Note: In the tab (and standard) notation in this book, a slur (a bent line) associating ascending notes indicates a hammer-on—the slur associates the primary fret number, or note, of the hammer-on with the second. If more than two ascending notes are slurred, all the notes after the first are hammered.

Playing a hammer-on

An open-string hammer-on (or simply hammer, for short) is the easiest kind to play. Following are the means for the open-string hammer-on,

1. Pick the open G string (the third string) as you normally do.

2. While the open string is as yet ringing, utilize a finger of your left hand (say, the first finger) to rapidly and immovably strike (or slam or smack, as you like) the second fret of the same string. If you carry your finger down with enough power, you hear the new note (the 2nd fret A) ringing. Usually, your left-hand doesn't strike a fret; it only presses beneath it. But to produce a clear sound without picking, you should hit the string entirely hard, as, however, your finger's a little hammer descending on the fretboard.

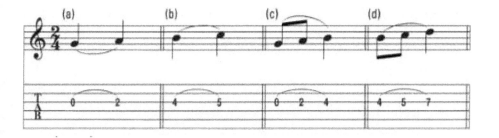

Image 23

The figure above shows a hammer-on from a fretted note on the third string. Utilize your first finger to fret the main note at the fourth fret and strike the string; at that point, while that note's despite everything ringing, utilize your second finger to hammer down on the fifth fret.

Sounding Smooth with Pull-Offs

Like a hammer-on, a draw off is a procedure that enables you to interface notes all the more quickly. It enables you to play two back to back dropping notes by picking just a single time with the correct hand and, as the first note rings, removing your finger off that fret. As you remove your finger off one fret, the following lower fretted (or open) note on the string at that point rings out instead of the primary note. You can think about a draw off as kind of something contrary to a hammer-on, but that particular contrast doesn't tell the entire story. A draw off also necessitates that you apply a slight sideways draw on the string where you're fretting the picked note and then discharge the string from your finger in ease as you remove your finger off the fret something like what you do in starting a tiddly-wink. Note: The tab (and standard) notation in this book indicates a pull-off by showing a slur associating (at least two) plunging tab numbers (or notes). The accompanying areas show all of you have to think about interfacing notes with the draw-off procedure, and when you're finished reading the means and licks, we give, you just may have the option to pull it off.

Playing pull-offs

A draw off (or pull, for short) to an open string is the easiest kind to play. Following are the means for the open-string pull-off

1. Press down the third string at the second fret with your first or second finger (whichever is increasingly comfortable) and pick the note normally with your correct hand.

2. While the note is as yet ringing, pull your finger off the string in a sideways movement (toward the second string) such that causes the open third string to ring just as if you're making a left-hand finger fortitude. If you're playing up to pace, you can't cull the string as you expel your finger; you're half lifting and half culling or somewhere in the middle. Test to locate the left-hand finger movement that works best for you.

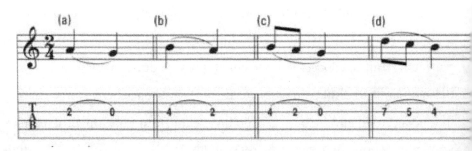

Image 24

The figure above shows a draw off, including just fretted notes. The crucial factor in playing this sort of pull-off is that you should finger both draw off-notes *ahead of time*. We set that last part in italics because it's so important. This necessity is one of the enormous differences between a hammer-on and a draw off. You should anticipate, or set up, a draw off in advance. Following are the means for playing the fretted draw off:

1. Press down both the 2nd fret of the third string with your first finger and the 4th fret of the 3rd strand with your third finger at the same time.

2. Strike the third string with the pick and, while the fourth fret note is as yet ringing, pull your third finger off the 4th fret (in half bravery, half lift) to sound the note of the 2nd fret (which you're already fingering).

3. Try to avoid accidentally striking the second string as you pull off. Moreover, if you aren't already pushing down that second fret note, you wind up pulling off to the open string rather than second fret! After you get the hang of the previous draw offs, you can take a stab at the twofold draw off and the twofold stop pull-off in the following segments.

The twofold draw off

Start by simultaneously fretting the initial two notes at the second and fourth frets (with your first and third fingers, separately). Take the string and then draw out with your third finger to sound the note at the second fret; at that point, pull off with your first finger to sound the open string.

81

The twofold stop pull-off

You can also play pull-offs as twofold stops. As is valid with hammer-ons, the most well-known and easiest to play twofold stop pull-offs are those where both twofold stop notes lie on the same fret, enabling you to bar them. Lay your first finger at the 2nd fret, barring the second and third strings, and set your 3rd finger at the 4th fret (also barring the second and third strings) at the same time. Pick the strings and then draw your third finger off the fourth fret to sound the notes at the second fret of the two strings. Presently attempt a twofold stop pull-off on the same strings.

Slipping Around with Slides

A slide is an articulation procedure where you play a note and then rotate your left-hand finger along the string to a separate fret. This procedure enables you to combine at least two notes easily and rapidly. It also allows you to change positions on the fretboard seamlessly. Many different sorts of slides are conceivable. The most basic incorporate those in the accompanying rundown (we show you how to master these slides, except maybe the last one, in the segments that follow):

- Slides between two notes where you pick just the main note.

- Slides between two notes where you pick the two notes.

- Slides from an uncertain pitch a couple of frets above or underneath the target note. (The pitch is uncertain because you start the slide with almost no finger pressure, gently increasing it until you arrive on the target fret.)

- Slides to an uncertain pitch a couple of frets above or beneath the starting note. (The pitch is uncertain because you gradually release finger pressure as you move away from the starting fret.)

- Slides into the home plate.

Note: In the tab (and standard) notation, we indicate a slide with a slanted line (in the case of approaching a note, interfacing two notes, or following a note).

Playing slides

The name of this method, slide, provides you an entirely decent insight into how to play it. You slide a left-hand finger upward or downward a string, maintaining contact with it, to arrive at the different note. Sometimes, you interface two notes (for example, you slide from the seventh fret to the ninth), and sometimes you associate a note (at a given fret) with an inconclusive pitch (you produce uncertain pitches by picking a string while you gradually add or release finger pressure as you're sliding). We portray the two strategies in the accompanying segments.

Connecting two notes

The slur means that this is a legato slide, which indicates that you don't pick the subsequent note. Play the principal note at the ninth fret normally, holding the note for one beat. At beat 2, while the string is as yet ringing, rapidly slide your left-hand finger to the 12th fret, keeping full finger pressure all through the entire time. This action makes the note at the 12th fret to sound without being picked.

Working with inconclusive pitch What we call an immediate ascending slide is a speedy slide, not in musicality, that serves to decorate just one note and isn't something that you use to interface two different notes. Follow this means:

1. Start the slide from about three frets beneath the target fret (the 6th fret if the 9th fret is your target), utilizing minimal finger pressure.

2. As your finger slides up, gently increase your finger pressure along these lines, as you arrive at the target fret, you apply full weight.

3. Beat the string with the pick while your left-hand finger is in movement, somewhere between the beginning and target frets (the sixth and ninth frets, in this example).

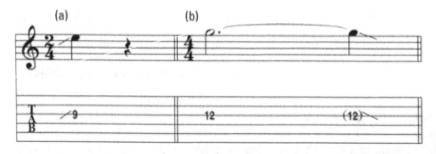

Image 25

Immediate ascending and plummeting slides; The slide shown in Figure above is what we call an immediate dropping slide. This sort of slide usually happens after you hold a note for some time. It gives a long note of a fancy consummation. Follow this means:

1. Pick the note that the tab shows (the one on the 12th fret in this case) in the normal way.

2. After letting the note ring for the designated duration, slide your left-hand finger down the string, gently release finger pressure as you go, to cause a fading-away impact. After a couple of frets, lift your finger totally off the string except if you want to play what's referred to as a long slide. In that case, you can glide your finger down the neck, releasing finger pressure (and finally expelling your finger from the string) toward the finish of the neck, as close to the nut as you want to go.

Stretching Out with Bends

More than any other sort of articulation, the **string twist** is what makes your guitar talk, make a sound (or sing or cry), giving the instrument almost voicelike expressive capabilities. Bowing is just utilizing a left-hand finger to push or haul a string out of its normal alignment, extending it across the fingerboard toward the sixth or first string, accordingly raising the pitch. As you twist a string, the ascent in pitch can be slight or great. Between the scarcest and greatest curves, conceivable are unending degrees off in the middle of twists. It's those interminable degrees that make your guitar sing.

Note: The tab notation in this book indicates a curve by utilizing a bent arrow and either a fraction of a number (or both) at the top of the arrow. The fraction ½, for example, means that you twist the string until the pitch is a half advance (the equivalent of one fret) higher than normal. The numeral 1 above a curve arrow means that you twist the string until the pitch is an entire advance (the equivalent of two frets) higher than normal. You may also observe fractions, for example, ¼ and ¾ or bigger numbers such as 1½ or 2 above a curve arrow. These fractions or numbers all reveal to you how many (entire) strides to twist the note. But ½ and 1 are the most widely recognized curves that you see in most tab notation. The standard notation in this book indicates a twist with a "pointed" slur associating the unbent pitch with the sounding (bowed) pitch

You can check that you're twisting in order by fretting the target note normally and comparing that to the bowed note. If the twist indicates an entire advance (1) on the seventh fret of the third string, for instance, play the 9th fret normally and listen care-completely to the pitch. At that point, take a stab at twisting the seventh fret note to match the ninth fret contribute your head. You don't usually do a lot of string bowing on acoustic guitars, because the strings are excessively thick. In electric guitar playing, where string bowing is an integral strategy, the strings are slenderer. In the accompanying areas, we show you bit by bit what you have to know to play twists, and we give you a couple of licks to practice.

Strings are estimated in gauges, with that term alluding to the diameter of the string in inches. A light-gauge set of acoustic strings begins with the width for the first string at 0.012 inches, which is generally viewed as unbendable by all aside from the most dedicated masochists. (Guitarists allude to the whole set in shorthand as twelves.) For electric guitars, the most well-known gauges start with sets that utilization a 0.009 or 0.010 gauge for the top string (nines and tens, to utilize the vernacular). You can twist with 0.011s and 0.012s (elevens and twelves) on your guitar, but doing so isn't a lot of fun except if you're really into pain!

Playing twists

You play this curve on the third string with the third finger, which speaks to a typical twisting situation probably the most well-known. Follow this means:

1. Place your 3rd finger at the 7th fret but support the 3rd finger by placing the 2nd finger at the 6th fret and the first finger at the fifth fret, all at the same time a). The 1st and second fingers don't produce any sound, but they add solidarity to your curve. Supporting your twists with any other available fingers is always a smart thought.

2. Pick the third string with your correct hand.

3. After picking, utilize all three fingers together to push the string toward the sixth string, raising the pitch an entire advance (to the pitch you normally get at the ninth fret Driving your hand around the neck as you perform the curve gives you added leverage. Also, utilizing light-gauge, or meager, strings on your guitar makes bowing easier.

Getting idiomatic with twists

In this area, you play several licks that feature a variety of twists, including the immediate curve, the twist in cadence, the twist and release, the held twist, and the twofold stop twist. We give you the details of each of these curves in the following segments.

Playing immediate curves in a stone performance Figure beneath shows a typical twist figure that you can use in rock soloing. Take note of the fingering that the standard notation staff indicates to utilize. Your left hand hardly moves; it's secured the fifth situation with the 1st finger barring the 1st also 2nd strings to the 5th fret. The 2nd notes of the figure (fifth fret, second string) happens to be the same pitch (E) as your target twist, so you can utilize that subsequent note to test the accuracy of your curve. Before long, you start to feel exactly how far you have to twist a string to achieve an entire advance or half-advance ascent in pitch. All the curves in this example are immediate twists.

Image 26; Bending the third string in a classic awesome lead lick.

After you play each third-string twist, not long before you pick the second-string note, diminish your finger pressure from the bowed note. This action causes the third string to quit ringing as you pick the second string.

Varying Your Sound with Vibrato

Think about the term vibrato, and you may imagine a vocalist's wavering voice or a musician's jerking hand. On the guitar, vibrato is steady, although (and usually slight) fluctuation of the pitch, frequently achieved by rapidly bowing and releasing a note a slight level. A vibrato can include warmth, emotion, and life to a held, or sustained, note. The most evident time to apply vibrato is at whatever point you hold a note for quite a while. That's the point at which you can add some emotion to the note

88

by utilizing vibrato. Vibrato gives the note more warmth, but it also increases the sustain time of the note. Some guitarists, for example, blues great B.B. Lord, are prestigious for their expressive vibrato procedure. Both the tab and standard notation shows a vibrato by placing a wavy line at the highest point of the staff over the note to which you apply the procedure. In the following areas, we portray different procedures for creating vibrato and give you some practice time with vibrato.

Methods for producing vibrato.

Vibrato can be produced in several ways:

1. You can marginally curve and release a note, again and again, creating a wah-wah-wah impact. The average pitch of the vibrato is a little bit higher than the unaltered note. The left-hand strategy for this technique is the same as the method for bowing you move a finger back and forward, perpendicular to the string, creating a fluctuation of the pitch.

2. You can rapidly slide your finger back and forward along the length of a string, inside one fret. Although you're not running your finger out of the fret, the pitch turns out to be marginally sharper as you advance toward the bridge and somewhat flatter as you advance toward the nut. Thus, the average pitch of the vibrato is the same as the unaltered note. This sort of vibrato is reserved almost solely for playing classical guitar with nylon cords.

If your electric guitar comes with a whammy bar located on it, you can move the bar all over with your correct hand, creating a fluctuation in pitch. In addition to giving you greater cadenced adaptability and pitch range, the whammy bar enables you to add vibrato to an open string.

Getting Mellow with Muting

To quiet notes or chords on the guitar, you utilize your privilege or left hand to contact the strings to partially or deaden the sound. You apply to quiet for one of the accompanying reasons:

- To create a thick, stout sound as an impact
- To keep unwanted clamors from strings that you're not playing
- To quiet annoying commercials on TV

The following segments show you how to utilize quieting and give a couple of passages to practice.

Creating a thick, stout sound as an impact

To utilize quieting to create percussive impacts, softly lay your left hand across all six strings to keep the strings from ringing out as you strike them. Try not to squeeze them down to the fretboard (which would cause the fretted notes to sound), but press them sufficiently hard to keep the strings from vibrating. At that point, hit the strings with the pick to hear the quieted sound. The tab notation indicates this kind of quieting by placing Xs on the string lines (and in place of the exact notes on the standard staff)

Playing a Song with Varied Articulation

"The Articulate Blues" is a short performance piece, as a 12-bar blues, that utilizes all the articulations we examine in this chapter. It consolidates single notes, chords, and riffs. It's a united style of playing that real-life guitarists use. Taking a gander at the song's notation, you see slides, pull-offs, twists, vibratos, and a hammer-on. The tab doesn't indicate any quieting, but you can utilize that procedure any time you want to avoid unwanted commotions; in measure 5, for example, you can lean your left thumb gently against the sixth string to keep it from ringing while you play the A7 harmony.

CHAPTER 09

ROCK GUITAR BASICS

laying Jammin guitar is arguably the best time you can have with an inanimate article in your hands. With the volume of your guitar turned up and your adrenaline streaming, nothing's very similar to laying down a piecing beat or tearing through a searing lead to screaming, adoring fans or even to your approving grin returning at you from the mirror.

You absorb it in simple, easy advances and then practice, practice, practice until it works out easily. After you get some beat and lead passages and get the methods down, the real work starts: standing before a mirror and culminating your moves.

Playing Classic Rock 'n' Roll.

Classic Jammin is characterized here as the simple style spearheaded by Chuck Berry in the music of the old Beatles, the Rolling Stones, the Who, the Beach Boys, and other people who based their sound on a strong, harmony-based mood guitar groove. It incorporates the sound of the blues-based rockers, for example, Jimi Hendrix, Led Zeppelin's Jimmy Page, and Cream's Eric Clapton. In the accompanying segments, we explain how to play both musicality guitar and lead guitar in the awesome classic style.

Musicality guitar

A lot of rock guitar playing includes what's known as mood guitar playing. To a guitarist, playing cadence means providing the backup or backing part to a vocalist or other featured instrument. Generally, this accompaniment includes playing chords and, to a lesser degree, playing single-note or twofold stop riffs in the lower register (the last a few strings). Tune in to the sections of Chuck Berry's "Johnny B. Goode" or the Beatles' "I Saw Her Standing There" for some great, unadulterated musicality guitar, and look at the Beatles' "Day Trip-per" for low-note riffing. Listen also to anything by the Who's Pete Townshend, who's (no joke proposed) the quintessential stone musicality guitarist and who immortalized the "wind-factory" procedure — the general circular movement of the correct hand to play chords. In the accompanying segments, we examine two elements of playing beat guitar: vacant position accompaniment and the 12-bar blues movement.

Vacant position accompaniment

The Chuck Berry style, which is a straightforward musicality figure (accompaniment pattern) in vacant position (utilizing open strings), earns its name from the fact that virtually all of Berry's songs utilize this pattern.

Lead guitar

After you gain a strong vibe for a basic Jammin cadence (see the previous area), you may want to attempt some lead guitar, which just includes playing single notes over a hidden accompaniment. You can play remembered licks, which are short, self-contained phrases, or you can

94

improvise by making up songs on the spot. In this segment, we give you the structure obstructs for great classic stone performances, assist you with blending in some articulation, show you how to string it all together, and wrap up with some tips on building your performances.

What's behind Box I? The pentatonic minor scale

You can play lead immediately by retaining a couple of straightforward pat-terns on the guitar neck, known as boxes, that produce instant outcomes. Guitarists retain a finger pattern that vaguely takes after the shape of a container, consequently the name box position, and use notes from that pattern (in various requests) again and again practically all through a performance or a segment of a performance. In soloing over a basic harmony movement, you can continue utilizing this one pattern regardless of whether the chords change. By learning the crates in this chapter, your arsenal for soloing over the 12-bar blues will be almost finished.

The first Box shown is made up of notes that are identified as the **pentatonic minor scale,** and it's the most helpful Box for exciting music. You don't have to consider hypothesis, scales, or chords, just the fingering, which you remember. These patterns contain no "off-base notes," so by ideals of simply moving your fingers around to a mood track, you can play instant Jammin lead guitar. You don't have to add water (which is naturally hazardous if you're playing an electric guitar).

The pentatonic minor scale has a five-note scale; its formula is measured in scale degrees (in comparison to a major scale that begins from the same note) is 1=3-4=5=7. If the notes on a C major scale, for instance, are numbered 1 through 7. The notes on the C pentatonic minor scale include C (1), E (3), F(4), G(5), B (7). That's the theory anyway, but for the time being, you're simply going to remember a pattern and utilize your ear — not your brain — to manage your fingers. **A** two-octave A pentatonic minor scale in 5th position. This instance is your first Box, here called **Box I.**

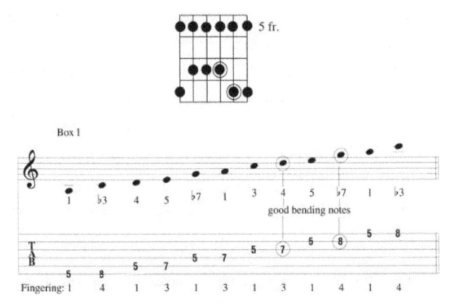

Image 27 Box I: A two-octave A pentatonic minor scale in the fifth position.

Before continuing, make sure you understand how the neck diagrams and staff relate. Note that the neck diagram doesn't show a harmony, but a scale, where the notes are played each in turn, from most minimal to most noteworthy (as shown in the standard notation and tab). We show you (below the notes in the usual notation) the scale degree (not all that important) and (below the tab numbers) the fingering (important) for each note; we also show you which notes are useful for bowing. Retain the fingering until you can play it in your rest. This pattern is necessary to know if you want to play rock guitar. Remember it. Do it. Play it again and again, all over. Really.

Having a crate to use in extemporizing lead guitar is what makes playing classic Jammin (or blues) so much fun; you don't have to think you just have a feel. You can't play only the five notes of the scale here and there, again and again — that would get exhausting exceptionally fast. Instead, you utilize your creativity to create licks by using the scale and adding articulations, for example, curves, slides, and hammer-ons, until you have a total performance.

Adding articulations

The case pattern shows you what to play, but articulations show you how to play. Articulations incorporate hammer-ons, pull-offs, slides, curves, and vibrato. These elements are what make a performance sound like a performance, give the independent articulation, and personalize it.

Bowing notes is probably the coolest sound in lead soloing, but the stunt realizes which notes to twist and when to do as such. When utilizing Box, I, guitarists prefer to twist notes on the second and third strings because the pressure feels right, and they get the chance to twist toward the roof their favorite course. Start by twisting the third finger note on the third string and the fourth finger note on the second string. Moving to Boxes A and B The following two boxes, which we name here Box A and Box B, don't show notes on all six strings as Box I does, because guitarists generally play just the notes on the best a few strings.

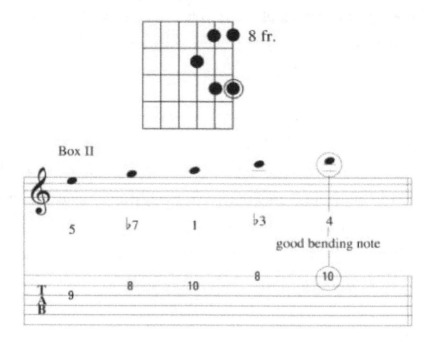

Image 28

Box A is popular because it features a decent note for bowing under the 3rd finger, and that note also occurs to be the most noteworthy in the container. In playing the lead, high is acceptable. You can play the most elevated note in the case and then make it considerably higher by twisting it up a stage. This strategy produces a significant dramatic impact. Attempt it. The figure underneath shows Box B (in the tenth situation for the key of A). Also, we show you the scale degree and fingering for each note, and we circle the note that's useful for bowing.

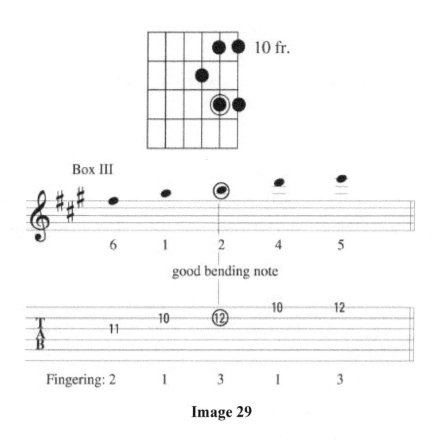

Box III

good bending note

Fingering: 2   1   3   1   3

Image 29

Building a solo by utilizing Boxes I, II, and III.

This area essentially assembles licks from the three boxes that we depict in the first areas. You needn't bother with any new information; you simply need to sort out what you understand if you study the information we give in those areas. (If you haven't yet, we recommend you do so now before you attempt the independent, we depict here.) simply after you make the blocks, can you set them up to make a house? Here, we show you how to manufacture a ready-made 12-bar solo comprising of six two-bar phrases (utilizing three boxes) that we show you in the first segments. Follow this means:

1. Play the Box I twofold stop lic

2. Play the Box I "bowing the third-string."

3. Play the Box III lick,

4. Play the Box I "bowing the second string" lick,

5. Play the Box II lick.

6. Play the Box I twofold stop lick again,

As you play this solo, again and again, you figure out soloing with the three boxes over a 12-bar blues movement. The great starts after you start making up your performances. Following are some rules for creating your leads:

1. Think as far as short phrases hung together. You can even play only one short phrase again and again, although the backing chords change. A decent way to compose a phrase is to make it a sing able and sweat one. Sing a short song in your mind, but use notes. Add some articulation, especially twists, because they sound the smoothest. Add vibrato to high notes that end a song, sometimes sliding down at the end.

2. Alternate among activity (lots of notes) and rest (a couple of notes or, on the other hand, only one note or even quiet for a couple of beats).

3. Slide from Box to box to give your performance some variety; Try not to be restrained or stress over making a mistake. In our sentiments, you can't make a mistake, because all the notes in the crates sound great against all the chords in the backing movement. The main mistake you can make is to avoid soloing for fear of sounding lame. Soloing takes practice, but you gradually

assemble certainty. If you're too modest to even think about soloing before individuals, start by doing it along with the audio tracks, where nobody can hear you. Soon, nobody can stop you. Tune in to accounts to get new ideas as you become increasingly sure about your playing. As you hear a chronicle, you may have the option to make sense of exactly what the guitarist is playing, because most guitarists utilize the same boxes, twists, vibratos, and so on that, you do.

Mastering Modern Rock

Whereas classical awesome cadence guitar utilizes straightforward chords, current exciting music makes utilization of chords different from basic major, minor, and seventh chords. Sus chords, slash chords, add chords, and unusual chords that come about because of retuning your guitar are all part of the cutting-edge rock language. These chords enable you to create completely new musicality guitar hues and surfaces that aren't conceivable in standard tuning. This sound was an especially important part of the '90s alternative development. We investigate the chords of the current stone in the accompanying segments.

Sus chords and add chords

Chords are regularly worked by taking each other note of a major scale. For example, if you construct a three-note harmony by taking each other note on the C major scale =(C=D=E=F=G-A=B), you get C=E=G (a C major harmony). The harmony individuals (the individual notes that make up the harmony) are named according to their scale levels: C is "1" (or the root of the harmony), E is "3" (or a third of the harmony), and G is

101

"5" (or a fifth of the harmony). In sus chords, you replace the 3rd of harmony with the fourth, as in sus4 (which you articulate "suss-four") or sometimes with the second, as in sus2. The subsequent sound is inadequate or uncertain but creates an intriguing sound that's neither major nor minor. An add harmony is a basic harmony, (for example, a major harmony) to which you add an extra note. If you take a C harmony and add a D note to it, for example, you have a Cadd2 (which you articulate "see-add-two") harmony (with notes C-D-E-G). This harmony is different from Csus2, which has no E. (The D had its spot.)

Drop-D tuning (DADGBE)

Drop-D tuning (alleged because you detune, or drop, the low E string down to D) is the alternate tuning that's nearest to standard tuning — you retune just the sixth string; so the open strings, from low to high, are D, A, D, G, B, E. To get into this tuning, lower (drop) your sixth string until it sounds an octave lower than your fourth string. This tuning allows you to play a D or Dm harmony with a low D as root on the sixth string, giving you a full, rich sound.

Open-D tuning (DADF#AD)

In an open tuning, the open strings usually structure a major harmony. In open-D tuning, they structure (huge amazement) a D harmony: from low to high, D, A, D, F, A, D. In this tuning, a large portion of the chords you play are only open strings or one finger barring across all six strings. You can, for example, play a G harmony essentially by barring the whole fifth fret with your first finger. Joni Mitchell has made broad utilization of this tuning in songs, for example, "Enormous Yellow Taxi." To get into this tuning, follow these means:

1. Drop your sixth string until it sounds an octave lower than the open fourth string.

2. Drop your third-string, so it matches the note at the fourth fret of the fourth string.

3. Drop your second string, so it matches the note at the third fret of the third string.

4. Drop your first string, so it matches the note at the fifth fret of the second string.

The pentatonic major scale

You can characterize the notes of the pentatonic minor scale in any key are 1, =3=4=5=7, as related to the major parent scale. You practice the scale as a retained box, which is okay. The pentatonic major scale, then again, utilizes the 1=2=3=5=6 notes of the major parent scale. It's a 5-note scale that has no chromatic modifications (that is, notes that you alter by raising or bringing down a half advance), so it sounds simply like a major scale with two notes forgot about. Again, the pentatonic major scale is helpful because it practically makes the music itself, and you can't play any "off-base" notes.

After you study the pentatonic minor scale, the pentatonic major scale is a simple. Simply move the pentatonic minor scale down three frets and presto, you have a pentatonic major scale. Play the same pattern, and the notes, hypothesis, and all that nonsense take care of themselves. Say, for example, that you realize that you play the A pentatonic minor scale at the fifth fret against a harmony movement in the key of A. Well, lay that lead pattern down to the 2nd position (where your left-hand forefinger plays the notes on the 2nd fret). You end up having an A pentatonic major scale, proper for nation rock and Southern-rock movements.

Taking a look at general ideas

Though you play electric blues in many keys by utilizing movable boxes), you play acoustic blues (sometimes called Delta Blues) in an empty position (usually playing low on the neck and combining open strings and fretted notes), most always in the key of E. The accompanying segments portray the basics you have to play acoustic blues.

Playing the tune and the accompaniment simultaneously

The basic brain behind acoustic blues is that you're playing an independent that incorporates both the tune (which you regularly extemporize) and the accompaniment at the same time. This technique is inverse that of electric blues, where one guitarist plays the tune (the lead) while another guitarist plays the accompaniment (the musicality). The substance of the style is as per the following: Your right-hand thumb plays the root of each harmony (the note the harmony is named after) in steady quarter notes on the bass strings.

Meanwhile, your right-hand fingers play song notes that you take from the E pentatonic minor scale or the E blues scale, in the vacant position.

The Power of Slide Guitar

Slide guitar is an important addition to blues-guitar strategy. In playing slide, you don't utilize your left hand to fret the guitar by squeezing the strings to the fretboard, as usual. Rather, you hold a metal or glass bar (the slide) across the neck and stop (abbreviate the vibrating length) the strings by squeezing the slide daintily against the strings at a given fret. To play in order, you should situate the slide legitimately over the fret wire itself, not after it as you do in normal fretting.

Utilizing a Capo

A capo is a gadget that clamps down across the fingerboard at a certain fret. Capos can operate by use of elastic, springs, or even threaded screws, but they all fill the same need — they abbreviate the length of all the strings at the same time, creating, basically, another nut. All the "open" strings presently play in higher pitches than they manage without the capo.

Tackling the Thumb-Brush Technique

The thumb-brush procedure is an accompaniment pattern that has a "blast chick" sound. Here, the thumb usually plays (culling a bass string downward), but the fingers strike (brush) the best three or four strings with the backs of the nails in a downward movement (toward the floor). The fingers play the strings as a pick does, but you don't move your arm or your entire hand. You twist your fingers into your palm and then rapidly expand them, changing from a shut hand position to an open-hand position, hitting the strings with the nails all the while.

CHAPTER 10

CHANGING YOUR STRINGS

A ny individuals believe their guitars to be delicate, valuable, and fragile instruments: They appear to be reluctant to tune their strings, not to mention them. Although you ought to be careful not to drop or scratch your guitar, you needn't stress over causing damage by changing, tuning, or overtightening guitar strings. The fact is that guitars are staggeringly rough and can deal with many pounds of string strain while persevering through the playing styles of even the most heavy-handed guitarists. Changing strings isn't something you ought to be timid about: You can bounce into it with the two feet. The task is similar to bathing your canine it's useful for the pooch, you're glad you did it, and it offers you a chance to draw nearer to man's closest companion. Similarly, changing your guitar strings scarcely has any drawbacks it improves the sound of the guitar, assists with forestalling broken strings at unfavorable minutes, and aids you in identifying other maintenance issues. During intermittent string changing, for example, you may find a gouged bridge slot or a free or rattling tuning post.

Hanging an Acoustic Guitar

Usually, steel-string acoustic guitars are easier to string than classical or electrics (which we spread in later segments in this chapter). In the accompanying segments, we walk you through the way toward changing an acoustic's strings, and we show you how to adjust it.

Stage 1: Attaching the string to the bridge

Acoustic guitars have a bridge with six gaps leading to within the guitar. To attach another string to the bridge, follow these means:

1. Remove the old string (see the earlier area "Evacuating Old Strings") and jump out the bridge pin.

2. Place the finish of the new string that has a little brass ring (called a ball) inside the opening that held the bridge pin. Simply stuff it down the opening a few inches. (How far isn't important, because you're going to pull it up shortly.)

3. Wedge the bridge pin solidly back in debt with the slot facing forward (toward the nut). The slot gives a channel to the string to get out

4. Pull delicately on the string until the ball leans against the base of the pin. Retain your thumb or finger on the pin so it won't jump out and disappear into the abyss.

5. Test the string by delicately pulling on it. If you can't feel the string shift, the ball is cozy against the bridge pin, and you're ready to tie down the string to the tuning post, which is the focal point of the accompanying segment.

Stage 2: Securing the string to the tuning post

After safely attaching the string to the bridge pin, you can concentrate on the headstock. The means are different for the treble strings (G= B=E) and the bass strings which are(E=A=D). You turn treble strings clockwise and bass strings anti-clockwise. Attaching a treble string to the tuning point, then follow this method:

1. Pass the string through the gap in the post. Give enough slack among the bridge pin and the tuning post to enable the string to wrap around the post multiple times when you adjust.

2. Kink (or crease) the metal wire toward within the guitar.

3. While retaining the string tight toward the post with one hand, wind the tuning peg clockwise with the other hand.

Tuning

Tuning an electric guitar isn't entirely different from tuning an acoustic (which we explain how to do earlier in this chapter). Again, the strings will sneak out of tune all the more easily and all the more frequently, so they'll require all the more tweaking to get all six strings up to pitch. If you have a floating bridge (depicted in the accompanying segment), tuning a string changes the pressure on the bridge, causing all the strings that were in the past to go somewhat off-key, so the procedure takes significantly more. But eventually, all the strings "settle down," and the tuning stabilizes.

Tuning up

After you ensure the string around the post and start twisting it with the tuning key, you can start to hear the string come up to pitch. As the string fixes, make sure it stays in its right nut slot. If you're changing strings each, in turn, you can simply tune the upgraded one to the old ones, which, presumably, are relatively in order. After you get the string to the right pitch, pull on it (by hauling it out and away from the fingerboard) in various places all over its length to extend it a piece. Doing so can make the string to go flat sometimes drastically if you left any free windings on the post so adjust it back to pitch by winding the peg. Repeat the tune-stretch procedure a few times to enable the new strings to hold their pitch.

Trigging a Nylon-String Guitar Stringing

A nylon-string guitar is different from hanging a steel-string acoustic because both the bridge and the posts are completely different. Nylon-string guitars don't utilize bridge pins (strings are tied off instead), and their headstocks are slotted and have rollers, as operation presented to posts. In the accompanying segments, we portray the means of changing the strings of a nylon-string guitar, and we explain how to adjust it changing strings bit by bit. In general, nylon strings are easier to handle than steel strings are, because nylon isn't as wiry as steel. Joining the string to the tuning post can be somehow trickier. As you do with the steel-string acoustic that we talk about earlier in this chapter, start by making sure about the bridge end of the string first and then direct your concentration toward the headstock.

Stage 1: Attaching the string to the bridge, whereas steel-string acoustic strings have a ball toward one side, nylon strings have no such ball: Both closures are free. (Well, you can purchase ball-finished nylon-string sets, but they're not what you normally use.) You can, in this manner, attach either end of the string to the bridge. If the closures appear to be unique, however, utilize the one that resembles the center of the string, not the one with the approximately curled appearance. Simply follow this means:

1. Remove the old string, as we depict in the segment " Pass one finish of the new string through the opening in the highest point of the bridge, toward the path away from the sound hole, leaving about 1½ inches standing out the rear of the opening.

2. Secure the string by producing the short end over the bridge and passing it under the long part of the string

3. Then pass the short end under, finished, and then under itself, on the highest point of the bridge

4. Pull-on the long finish of the string with one hand and move the hitch with the other to evacuate abundance slack and cause the bunch to lie flat against the bridge.

Hanging an Electric Guitar

Usually, electric guitarists require to change their strings more regularly than do steel-string acoustic or nylon-string guitarists. Because changing strings is so regular on electric guitars, manufacturers take an increasingly dynamic approach to the hardware, frequently making changing strings extremely speedy and easy. Of the three sorts of guitars — steel-string acoustic, nylon-string, and electric you can replace the strings on electric guitars most easily by a wide margin.

We explain how to change an electric's strings and tune it up in the accompanying segments. Changing strings bit by bit. As you would on steel-string acoustic and nylon-string guitars (the two of which we spread earlier in this chapter), start hanging an electric guitar by first tying down the string to the bridge and then attaching the string to the headstock. Electric strings are related to steel-string acoustic strings in that they have ball closes and are made up of metal. Still, electric strings are normally made out of a lighter gauge wire than steel-string acoustic strings, and the third-string is loosened up, or plain, whereas a steel-string acoustic guitar is wound. (A nylon-string's third-string usually is loosened up but is a thicker nylon string.)

Stage 1: Attaching the string to the bridge

Most electric guitars utilize a basic strategy for tying down the string to the bridge. You pass the string through a gap in the bridge (some-times fortified with a collar or grommet) that is lesser than the ball at the finish of the string so the ball holds the string similarly as the bunch at the finish of a bit of thread holds a line in the fabric. On some guitars, (for example, the Fender Telecaster), the collars anchor directly into the body, and the strings move through the back of the instrument, through a gap in the bridge assembly, and out the top. Figure 18-6 shows two plans for attaching a string to an electric: from a top-mounted bridge and through the back. The accompanying advances show how to tie down the strings to the bridge.

1. Remove the old string, as discussed," earlier.

2. Tie the string at the bridge, bypassing the string through the opening (from the back or base of the guitar) until the ball stops the development. At that point, you're ready to concentrate onthe tuning post.

Stage 2: Securing the string to the tuning post In many cases, the posts on an electric look like those of a steel-string acoustic. A post juts through the headstock, and you pass your string through the post's opening, crimp the string to within (toward the focal point of the headstock), and start winding while at the same time holding the long part of the string with one hand for control.

CONCLUSION

There are no alternate ways to mastering guitars. No beginner can learn guitar by simply reading an exercise or watching a video. A maturing guitarist must grab a guitar and practice the same exercise repeatedly until it turns into a natural activity.

Learn the barre chords straightaway by composing a decent song and study any new chords. Practice each day and enjoy it! Where to go from here knowing the chords will make you a good guitarist. The individuals who want to play guitar performances ought to learn guitar scales.

While harmony charts determine what combination of strings to press to shape a harmony, a guitar scale determines what individual strings to press to create guitar performances. Guitar performances are the instrumental part heard on certain songs. The pentatonic scale is the easiest to learn, utilizing just five notes out of the seven notes of the major scale. Realizing the pentatonic scale is the initial step to guitar improvisation. Retaining the pentatonic scale and realizing how to utilize it allows the guitar player to create guitar performances on the spot.

MUSIC THEORY

How to UNDERSTAND And LEArn Music for
GuiTAR, PIANO AND Others MusiCAL
Instruments

(Revised Edition)

TABLE OF CONTENT

INTRODUCTION

What comes to your mind when you hear the word music theory? Does the image of your primary school music teacher peer toward you from behind the piano fly into your head? Or then again perhaps you have flashbacks to a later image of individual understudies in theory classes firmly attempting to note the whistles? If both ideas are anything near your impression of what music theory is, ideally, this book will be a pleasant shock. For a lot of self-taught musicians, the thought of theory appears to be daunting and even somewhat self-defeating. Overall, if at the moment, you can read guitar keys and play some scales, for what reason would you want to obfuscate what you already know with theory? Even the most basic music theory training gives you the information you need to expand your range and abilities as a musician. An OK amount of note-reading ability enables you to play a particular music. In contrast, some basic information about harmony movements can assist you with composing your music.

CHAPTER 01

WHAT IS MUSIC THEORY

O ne of the most important things to recollect about music theory is that music is inertial. Music has being in existence for thousands of years before theory came along to explain what individuals were attempting to accomplish when beating on their drums. So, absolutely never feel that you can't be a decent musician because you've never taken a theory class. If you are a decent musician, you probably know a lot of theory, although you may not know the wording or technicalities. The ideas and decides that makeup music theory is a lot of like the grammatical standards that administer composed language (which also came along after individuals had successfully found how to talk to each other). Similarly, as being able to transcribe language made it workable for individuals far away to "hear" conversations and stories the way the author expected, being able to transcribe music allows musicians to read and play pieces exactly as the arranger planned. Learning music is fun, like learning another language, to where a familiar individual can "hear" a musical "conversation" when reading a bit of sheet music.

A lot of individuals on the planet can't read or compose, but they can even now communicate their thoughts and feelings verbally fine and dandy. Similarly, a lot of natural, self-taught musicians have never learned to read or compose music and locate the entire idea of learning music theory dull and unnecessary. However, much the same as the educational leaps that can accompany learning to read and compose. Music theory can assist musicians with mastering new strategies, perform unfamiliar styles of music, and build up the certainty they have to attempt new things.

Putting the Spotlight on Music Theory Fundamentals

While it is pleasant to be one of those individuals who can sit at any instrument and play beautiful music with no training, most people need some kind of organized guidance, regardless of whether from a teacher or from reading a book. In the accompanying segments, we go over the basic information you need to study music, play scales, understand key signatures, and assemble harmonies.

Understanding the foundation: The Notes, rests, and beats

Learning how to understand music is vital to a musician, especially one who wants to share his music with different musicians or find what different musicians are playing. By examining the basic elements, for example, time values of each kind of composed note, musical rests, time signatures, and beat you put yourself on the path to mastering music. All these elements meet up to establish a foundation that allows you to read, play, and study music.

Manipulating and merging notes

Reading musical notes on each treble and bass clef staves and discovering notes on the piano and guitar — the two most regular instruments on which individuals teach themselves to play are crucial to making and considering music. At the point when you can read notes on the staves, you can decide a musical piece's key signature, which is a group of images that mentions to you what key that they write such a melody in. You can use the Circle of Fifths to help train yourself to read key signatures immediately by including the sharps or flats in a period signature. After you've gotten comfortable with key signatures, you're ready to proceed toward intervals, harmonies, and harmony movements, which create the multifaceted nature of musical sound — from pleasing and calming to tense and needing goals.

Contemplating musical structure and synthesis

They create popular and classical music using specific structures. A structure is a structural outline used to create certain music. The structure squares of structure incorporate musical phrases and periods, and mood, tune, and harmony enter the image to create the class, or style, of a bit of music. When plunking down to compose music, pick the structure you want to follow (for example, classical and popular). You can browse different classical and popular structures, including sonatas, concertos, 16-bar blues, and section tune structure. You can create varied sounds in whatever structure you pick by playing with rhythm, dynamics, and instrument tone shading.

Perceiving How Theory Can Help Your Music

If you didn't know better, you can imagine that music was something that could start on any note, go anyplace it wanted, and stop at whatever point the entertainer wanted to get up for a glass of frosted tea. Although, the facts confirm that many people have been to musical performances that follow this style of synthesis and these performances are befuddling and annoyingly self-liberal and feel somewhat silly. The main individuals who can pull off a spontaneous jam well are the individuals who know music altogether enough to stack harmonies and notes by each other, so they make sense to audience members. And, because music is innately a communication, interfacing with the member of your audience is the goal.

Understanding Musical Tones

So what's a tone? The definition is straightforward: a tone is a sound that is played or sung at a specific pitch. At the point when you murmur (proceed), you're murmuring a tone. At the point when you whistle, you're whistling a tone. At the point when you go, "aaaahhhh," you sound a tone. If you put at least two murmurs, whistles, or "aaaahhhhs" together, you have music. You can murmur lots of different tones, high or low. We allude to the higher tones as **sharp sounding**; we call lower tones the lower-pitched.

> ▸ **Here's an activity:** Hum a tone. Murmur a tone higher than the primary tone. What you've recently whispered are two separate tones, at two separate pitches. The second tone was shriller than the principal tone. Different voices, and unusual instruments, produce various ranges of tones. For instance, ladies will have higher voices than men; the tones most ladies sing are shriller than the tones most men sing. (There are exceptional cases to this standard, obviously; hear some out of the doo-wop vocalists of the 1950s, and you'll hear some reasonably high male voices!) In the realm of musical instruments, physically larger

instruments will produce lower-pitched tones, whereas smaller instruments will, in usual, provide sharp sounding tones. This is because greater instruments move more air than smaller ones do, and more air means a lower pitch. This is the reason the small chamber of a woodwind produces higher notes than the enormous brass tubing of a tuba, and why the dainty strings on a guitar are sharp sounding than the thick strings. Other instruments produce a broader range of tones than different instruments. In particular, the piano has a comprehensive range. From the most minimal tone (the key on the far left of the keyboard) to the most elevated (the key on the far right), the piano imitates a greater number of tones than pretty much any other instrument—and surely a lot more than the human voice!

▸ **Time for another activity:** Hum the most reduced tone you can murmur; at that point, gradually raise the pitch until you're whispering the most noteworthy tone you can murmur. You just whispered a mess of different tones. How, at that point, do you portray a specific tone with the goal that someone else can murmur the same tone?

Tones Have Value

Regarding portraying a tone, it assists with realizing that each tone you can sing or play has a specific value. You can measure that value scientifically, and use that value to depict the tone—or, all the more correctly, its pitch. If that's as well complicated, you also can give an arbitrary name to each ton.

What's the Frequency?

If you plug a receiver into an oscilloscope and then murmur a tone into the amplifier, the oscilloscope will measure the frequency in the tone. This is usually a measurement of how fast the atoms of air are vibrating; the faster the vibrations, the higher the pitch. We measure these vibrations in cycles every second, and there are a lot of them. (We regularly call Cycles every second hertz; abbreviated Hz.) If you murmur the pitch, we call middle C (the white key in the exact focal point of a piano keyboard, or the third fret on the A string of a guitar), the oscilloscope will measure 256Hz—that is, the air is cycling back and forward 256 times each second. So, one perfect way to identify specific pitches is by their frequency. Unfortunately, working out even a basic tune regarding frequency gets a tad cumbersome. For example, here's the main half of Mary Had a Little Lamb= ("Mary had a little lamb, little lamb, and little lamb") denoted 'g' by frequency:

659Hz=587Hz= 523Hz=587Hz=659Hz=659Hz, 659Hz=

587Hz= 587Hz=587Hz,

659Hz=783Hz=783Hz

The definite frequencies of **"Mary Had a Little Lamb."**

It's difficult to read, right? That is the reason we don't use the frequency technique to compose music.

Play by each Number

A perfect way to designate tones is to number each pitch. But previously, we figure; it assists with knowing a tad about how different pitch relates to each other. At the point when you murmur a pitch, you can "slide" that pitch from lower to higher and back again, which may make you feel that there is an endless number of pitches available. (You can observe this when you take a gander at frequencies; you have one tone at 256Hz, another at 257Hz, another at 258Hz, and so on.)

Although that may be valid in theory while in practical, some pitches are excessively close together to recognize them. For example, if you murmur a 256Hz tone, 257Hz tone, they sound almost identical in pitch because there isn't a major enough interval between the tones. We have to place a reasonable interval between tones, enough for our ears to notice, and then assign values to those main pitches that outcome. What you end up with is a sequence of pitches called a **scale**. Each scale begins on a specific tone and finishes on a shriller rendition of that same tone.

In the Western world, we partition our scales into seven main notes— eight if you tally the main note, which is repeated at the end of the scale. Because there are seven notes, it's easy to number them—one through seven. Using this numbering system, here is what the first half of "Mary Had a Little Lamb" resembles:

3 2 1 2 3

2

3 5

Mary Had a Little Lamb; by numbers

If you're studying ahead and want to perceive how the numbering system applies to traditional music notation, by the numbers, this is what the C Major scale resembles:

Fig: Numbering the notes in the C Major scale.

Not to be confounding here, but there are notes between some of these main notes—enough of them we have twelve pitches before they rehearse. These, in the middle of contributes, are equally spaced what we call half advances, where the major pitches (A, B, C, and so on.) have. It is possible that two half strides between them, contingent upon the note. (I know, it's getting befuddling already).

We will concentrate on the seven main notes of a scale, since that's very easy to understand.

Do Re Mi

Another way to recollect each tone is by assigning a straightforward syllable to each tone. Recollect the melody from the Sound of Music that goes "**Do a deer, a female deer**" -- that's what we're talking about here. We call it Solfeggio or Solfege (articulated sol-FEZH) and each of the seven notes of a scale has its name. The accompanying table shows the applicable words.

The Solfeggio Method

Tone	Solfeggio name	Pronunciation
1	Do	Doh
2	Re	Ray
3	Mi	Mee
4	Fa	Fah
5	So (Sol)	So
6	La	Lah
7	Ti	Tee
8	Do	Doh

Table 1: The Solfeggio Method

This is what the main half of "Mary Had a Little Lamb" looks like using the Solfeggio strategy:

Mi Re Do Re Mi

Re

Mi So

"Mary Had a Little Lamb" in Solfeggio

If you're reading advanced music and want to understand how the Solfeggio names apply to traditional music notation, this is what the C Major scale resembles:

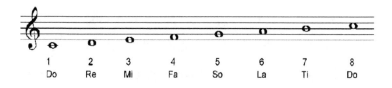

Fig 2: The Do Re Mis of the C Major scale.

Tones have different Names

It's important to realize that both the numbering and the Solfeggio techniques are relative ways of naming musical tones, i.e. the main note in a scale is always number one, and we call it Do. The subsequent tone is always number two and is always called Re. It doesn't make a difference what actual tone you start with; these names always apply. The issue with using relative naming is that it doesn't mention to you the exact pitch to start with. You may start your Do Re Mi on a low pitch, and your neighbor may start his/hers on a higher pitch, and your two-part harmony will wind up sounding like two water buffaloes in heat; that's bad. (Except if you're a water buffalo, obviously.) No, what we need is a way to differentiate specific pitches—without turning to the cumbersome frequency strategy.

Learning the ABCs

The perfect way of naming specific musical pitches uses the initial seven letters of the alphabet—A, B, C, D, E, F, and G. While the numbering technique is relative (the number 1 can be assigned to any pitch), the letter technique is absolute. This means that it alludes to a specific frequency. At the point when you tell someone to sing or play an A, they'll always sing or play the same pitch. The main issue with this strategy is that you can sing or play over one A. Attempt this activity: Sing A B C D E F G A (think "Do Re Mi Fa So La Ti Do"). The initial An and the second An ought to be the same tone, with the second An octave higher than the initial A. (You'll learn about octaves in the later chapter— get the job done to say it's a way of introducing a lower or higher variant of the same note.) We can play

Note A with a low pitch, and A with a higher pitch—and different As both beneath and above those. All the as will have the same tone; they're sequential forms of the basic pitch. How, at that point, do you advise which A to play or sing?

Notes on a Piano Keyboard

A decent way to visualize the seven basic notes (A through G) is to take a gander at a piano keyboard. Each white key on the keyboard relates to one of these seven main notes, as shown in the accompanying figure. (And overlook the black keys, until further notice.)

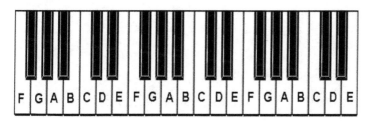

Fig 3: The white keys on a piano keyboard.

As you can see, the black and white keys on a piano arrangement follow a certain pattern. If you start in the ideal place, you'll see that they arrange the black keys in groups of threes and twos. We always assign the main white key to one side of a group of three black notes to the tone of F. They usually assign the primary white key to one side of a group of two black notes to C. When you know where F and C are, you can make sense of the location of different tones. To make sense of which An (or F or C) to play, realize that the C is in the very middle of the piano keyboard—straightforwardly underneath the manufacturer's logo or then again pull-down entryway handle—is called middle C. (It's the C in the middle of the keyboard; easy to recollect.) we can depict All different notes relative to middle C—as in "the F above middle C" or "the D beneath middle C."

Notes on a Staff

Since you know the seven basic notes and where they lie on a piano keyboard, how would you approach communicating those notes to other people? You could illuminate a melody; if you use this technique, the principal half of "Mary Had a Little Lamb" would resemble this:

E D C D E

D

E G

The notes: Mary Had a Little Lamb

That's more specific than using numbers or Solfeggio, but it's still somewhat difficult to read. A superior way to note pitches is to do so visually, using a graphic that, in some ways, takes after a basic piano keyboard. This graphic is called a staff. They make the basic music staff from lines and spaces in this way:

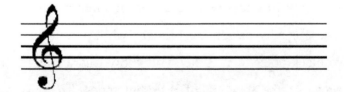

Fig 4: A blank staff.

As you can see, the staff has exactly five lines and four spaces. Each line or space speaks to a specific pitch. The clef dictates the pitches at the start of the staff; the staff we're taking a gander at here utilizations what we call the treble clef.

Fig 5: The notes of a staff (Treble Clef).

This treble clef staff shows the notes in the exact middle of a piano keyboard just above middle C. (The bottom line of the staff speaks to the E above middle C.) The accompanying figure shows how the notes of the staff relate to specific piano keys.

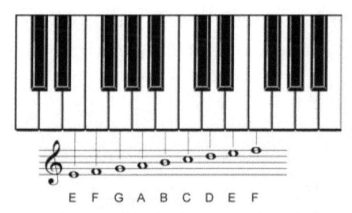

Fig 6: Notes in the exact middle of a piano keyboard just above middle C

The notes on the staff and the place they appear on a piano keyboard. Back to "Mary Had a Little Lamb"; this is what the initial segment of that tune looks like on a music staff:

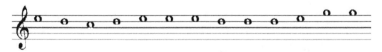

Fig 7: The notes "Mary Had a Little Lamb" on a music staff.

Above—and Below—the Staff

The basic staff portrays nine basic notes, which are five on the lines and four in the spaces. But what of all the notes either above or beneath these nine notes—that was last notes in "Mary Had a Little Lamb"?

The Notes that are higher than the F at the highest point of the staff are written in the lines and spaces above the staff. For example, the principal space above the staff is the first note after F: G. The primary line above the staff is the main note after G: A. You can continue adding spaces and lines above the staff to depict increasingly elevated notes. Similarly, as you can add lines and spaces above the staff, you can also add lines and spaces beneath the staff to portray lower notes. For example, the main space beneath the staff is the first note before E: D. The mainline underneath the staff is the primary note before D: C. The accompanying figure shows the initial few notes underneath the standard staff. Coincidentally, the primary line beneath the staff is middle C.

Fig 8: Notes underneath the Staff.

Different Clefs

Up till now, we've been talking about the gander at a staff that speaks to the notes just above middle C on the piano keyboard. The notes of this staff are controlled by the kind of clef that appears at the beginning of the staff—and there are several kinds of clefs.

The Treble Clef

The clef we've been studying so far is called the treble clef; it would appear like this:

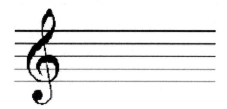

Fig 9: The treble clef.

As you've already learned, in real terms, we situate the treble clef just above middle C. The baseline of the treble clef staff is an E; the top line is an F. The treble clef, similar to all clefs, fixes the situation of a single pitch from which you can sense where all the remaining the notes go. On account of the treble clef, the pitch it sets is G, which is the next line on the staff. (If you look intently at the treble clef itself, you will see that the large round part of the clef circles around the second line of the staff.) For this purpose, we seldom call the treble clef the **G clef**—and the clef itself looks similar to a capital G.

If you ever have inconvenience recalling which note goes with line or space on staff, here's an easy way to recollect them. We locate the lines for the treble clef staff, bottom to top, to the notes E, G, B, D, and F. You can recollect the lines by recollecting the first letters in the phrase "Each Good Boy Deserve Food." We then ascribe the areas of the treble clef staff, bottom to top, to the notes F, A, C, and E. You can recollect the spaces by recalling "FACE." More shrill instruments and voices use the treble clef. This incorporates trumpets, woodwinds, clarinets, and guitars, and artists singing the soprano, alto, and tenor parts.

The Bass Clef

At the point when you have to compose music beneath the treble clef, you can use a different clef, called the bass clef. The bass clef is situated just beneath middle C and is sometimes referred to as the **F** clef. (That's because the two dabs on the clef encompass the fourth line, which is F.) This is what the bass clef resembles, with the notes of a bass clef staff:

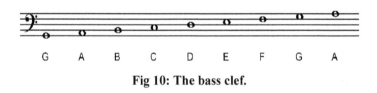

Fig 10: The bass clef.

Most turn down the volume when using the bass clef. This incorporates trombones, tubas, bass guitars, and artists singing the bass part. An easy way to recollect the lines of the bass clef is with the phrase "Great Young men Do Fine Always." (The principal letter of each word portrays each line of the staff, from bottom to top.) To recall the spaces of the bass clef, recollect the primary letters in the phrase "All Cows Eat Grass."

The Grand Staff

If you play or compose for piano, there's another staff you have to know. This staff called the **grand staff** interfaces collectively a treble clef staff, and a bass clef staff. (That's because you play the piano with both hands; each staff relates to each hand. When you use a grand staff, it's essential to note that the two staff neatly stream into each other. Then the highest point of the bass clef reaches out preceding that staff to a B and a C. The C is then connected to the treble clef, goes on up to a D, and at that point the E on the bottom line of the treble clef. Interestingly, the C—which is middle C—is halfway between each staff. So when you compose a middle C on a grand staff, it may reach out down from the treble clef staff or stretch out up from the bass clef staff, contingent upon where they place the encompassing notes.

Specialty Clefs

There are a lot of specialty clefs you should learn, although you probably won't use them much. These clefs are intended for instruments whose range doesn't fit comfortably inside the traditional treble or bass clefs. One of the most well-known specialty clefs is the alto clef, shown here:

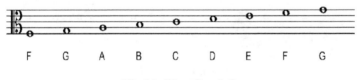

F   G   A   B   C   D   E   F   G

Fig 11: The alto clef.

The alto clef is used primarily by the viola, which is a somewhat greater form of a violin. The pointer on this clef focuses on the middle C, which is the third line in the specific middle of the staff.

The tenor clef is similar to the alto clef, except for the pointer focuses on a different line. (It, despite everything, focuses on middle C, but middle C is situated at a different point on the staff.) The tenor clef resembles this, and is sometimes used by bassoons, bass violins, and tenor trombones.

D   E   F   G   A   B   C   D   E

Fig 12 The tenor clef.

Although, there are several other special clefs (e.g. counting the sub-bass, baritone, and French violin clefs) but you probably won't run into them often; they're not generally used. However, you may run into what is called an octave clef, which resembles a normal treble or bass clef with the number 8 either above or beneath the clef. At the point when you see this kind of clef, you should transpose the usual treble clef notes both up (if the 8 is above the clef) or down (if the 8 is beneath the clef) an octave.

Fig 13: Octave Clefs

The Percussion Clef

There's a critical clef you should know, and it's the easiest of them all. We use this clef when you're composing for drums and other percussion instruments—those that don't play a fixed pitch. The great thing about this clef is that the lines and spaces don't compare to any specific pitches. Rather, you assign separate instruments to different parts of the staff. For instance, if you're composing for a drum set, you may assign the bass drum to the base space, the snare drum to the third space, and two tom-toms to the second and fourth spaces; you can put the ride cymbal on the top line of the staff.

CHAPTER 02

INTERVAL

o make things as basic as conceivable, we'll talk about these contributes and intervals terms of the C Major scale—that is, the notes between one C on the piano keyboard and the following C above that. We can apply the basic ideas to any scale, as you'll see; it's that adhering to a single scale which makes it all somewhat easier to understand. (And, at minimum one on the piano, the C Major scale is the simplest scale to work with—it's all white keys!)

Be Sharp or Be Flat, We can apply the basic ideas

The lines and spaces on a musical staff relate precisely to the white keys on a piano. But what about those black keys? Where are they on the staff? When we say there are 7 main keys contributing to a Western musical scale (A through G), that's a touch of an oversimplification: There are 12 potential notes in an octave, with some of them falling between the 7 main pitches. Tally the keys between middle C and next C on the piano—including the black keys, but without checking the subsequent C. If you counted accurately, you checked 12 keys, which speak to 12 pitches; each pitch/key is the same interval away from the past pitch/key.

We sometimes refer the black keys to as **sharps and flats.** The Sharps and flats are halfway among the pitches, spoke to by the white keys on a piano; a sharp is above a specific key, and a flat is underneath a specific key. Put another way, a sharp increase in the natural note; a flat lower the note. For instance, take the black key over the middle C key. You can allude to this key as C-sharp because it raises the pitch of C. We call this the D-flat because it brings down the following white key up, D. It may be a bit of befuddling, but its valid C-sharp is the same note as D-flat. And at whatever point, you have two notes that depict the same pitch—like C-sharp and D-flat—the notes are enharmonic. These are the double names you can use for a piano's black keys:

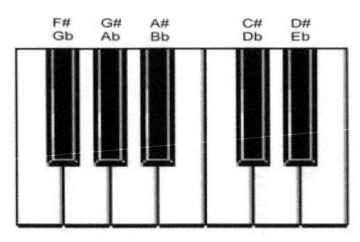

Fig 14: The black keys on a piano keyboard.

On a musical staff, sharps and flats are indicated by special characters placed before the affected note. These characters, called accidentals, and resemble this:

Fig 15: Sharp and Flat indictors

We call the third Character "A natural." At the point when you see a natural sign on a piece of music, it means to restore the specific note to its natural state, with no sharps or flats. Understand that you can include sharps and flats to any note—even those keys on a piano that don't have black notes between them. Along these lines, for example, if you add a flat to the C note, you lower it to the following note on the keyboard, that is, B neutral. The least interval in Western music is **the half advance**. On the piano keyboard, half advances appear between the white keys B and C, and among E and F. Altogether, different cases they appear between a white key and a black key—for example, D to D-sharp, or F-sharp to G.

A two-half advance equals one entire advance. The interval among F and G is an entirety step; the interval among B and C-sharp is also a complete advance one. Since you think about advances, it's somewhat easier to understand how sharps and flats work. At the point when you sharpen a note, you move the pitch up a half advance.

When a note is flattened, you move the pitch down a little towards half way

Take the note C, for instance: When you combine a flat to C, you take it down a half step. Because the primary key (white or black) to one side of C is the white key B, this means C-flat equals B. At the point when you add a sharp to C, you take it up a half step. The main key to one

141

side of C is the black key we call C-sharp. (This black key is also the principal key to one side of D, which means C-sharp is the same as D-flat.) You can use the progression strategy to depict the intervals between two notes. However, once you get over two steps away, the tallying turns into a tad difficult. At the point when you're attempting to make sense of which note is seven half strides above middle C (it's G, in case you're checking); it's a great opportunity to use another strategy to portray your intervals.

A Matter of Degrees

A progressively accepted way of portraying intervals is to return to the seven main notes of a scale, and get back to the relative numbering strategy. You can use the numbers of the scale to show the basic intervals among notes, and in this manner, apply this numbering to any scale.

First Thing first

As you learned in the past chapter, you can use numbers to depict the seven main notes on any scale. We number the main note as one, the subsequent note as two, and so on. This technique for numbering portrays the seven degrees of a musical scale. There also are beautiful musical names you can use in place of the numbers which you might encounter in some increasingly formal situations. The accompanying table presents these formal degree names.

Degrees of the Scale

Degree	Name
First (Root)	Tonic
Second	Supertonic
Third	Mediant
Fourth	Subdominant
Fifth	Dominant
Sixth	Submediant
Seventh	Leading Note
Eighth (Octave)	Tonic

Table 2: Scale Degrees

There are more terms you have to know before we continue. At the point when two different instruments or voices play notes of the same pitch, they're played as one. Two identical notes with the similar name played eight degrees apart structure an octave. (The word octave originates from the Latin word Octo, for "eight"—because an octave is eight notes above the starting note.) For instance, if you go from middle C to the following C up the keyboard, that's an octave; F to F is another octave, and so on. These musical degrees prove useful when you're portraying intervals between notes. Instead of tallying half advances and entire advances, you can portray an interval by utilizing these relative numbers (For example, suppose you want to depict the interval between C and D). If you consider C as the number one (the primary degree), D is number two, and we call the interval between them a second, the interval among C and E (the first and third degrees) is a third; the interval among C and F (the first and fourth degrees) is a fourth... and so on. It becomes easier when you are more committed to doing it!

Major and Minor Intervals

At the point when you depict intervals by degree, you, despite everything, have to deal with those pitches that fall above or beneath the basic notes, the sharps and flats keys, or the black keys on a keyboard. When estimating by degrees, you see that the second, third, 6th and seventh notes can be easily flattened. At the point when you flatten one of these notes, you create what we call a minor interval. The natural state of these intervals (on a major scale) is called a major interval. This is what these four intervals resemble, with C as the root, in both major and minor structures.

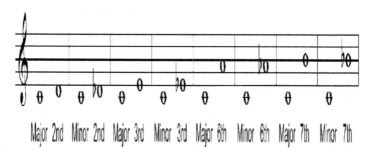

Major 2nd Minor 2nd Major 3rd Minor 3rd Major 6th Minor 6th Major 7th Minor 7th

Fig 16: The Resemblance of the Four Intervals

Perfect Intervals

Some intervals don't have different major or minor states (although they can still be flattened or sharpened). These intervals—fourths, fifths, and octaves exist in one structure called an ideal interval. You can't bring down these intervals to make them minor or raise them to make them major; there's nothing of such as a minor 5th or a major octave.

Here are the three flawless intervals, with C as the root;

Perfect   4th   Perfect   5th   Octave

Augmented and Diminished Intervals

Okay, now you realize that ideal intervals can't either be major or minor. That doesn't mean that you cannot change them. However, you can increase and lower fourths and fifths — and the outcome isn't called major or minor. At the point when you raise an ideal interval a half advance, it's called an augmented interval. At the point when you bring down an ideal interval, a half advance, it's called a diminished interval. So, don't refer to the new intervals as major or minor, instead call them augmented or rather diminished. For instance, if you use C as the root, F is an ideal fourth away from the root. If you sharpen the F, the following note (F-sharp) is an augmented fourth above the root. Along the same lines, G is an ideal fifth above C. At the point when you flatten the G, the coming about the note (G-flat) is a diminished fifth above the root. Below are the keys, expanded and diminished intervals, with C as the root.

Fig 18: Augmented and diminished intervals, starting on C.

Just to confound things, we can also call various kinds of intervals as diminished and augmented, and these intervals have nothing to do with the ideal intervals. To begin, you can also create a diminished interval by taking down a minor interval by another half advance. For instance, F to D-flat is a minor 6th; if you flatten the D-flat (truly, there's such an incredible concept as a double flat), we call the subsequent interval a diminished 6th. You can also make an augmented interval by raising a major interval by another half advance. For example, F to A will be a major third; if you sharpen the A (to A sharp), the subsequent interval is an augmented third. Luckily, you don't have to deal with either diminished or augmented interval that frequently. But you, despite everything, need to comprehend what they are if something goes wrong!

Past the Octave

You don't have to quit checking intervals when you get to the octave. Above the octave are much more intervals like ninths, tenths, elevenths, and more. We call the intervals that traverse more than an octave the **compound** intervals because they join an octave with a smaller interval to create a larger interval. For example, a ninth is just an octave and a second; an eleventh is an octave and a fourth, and so on. The accompanying table depicts the initial six intervals above the octave.

Compound Intervals

Interval	Combines
Ninth	Octave plus second
Tenth	Octave plus third
Eleventh	Octave plus fourth
Twelfth	Octave plus fifth
Thirteenth	Octave plus sixth
Fourteenth	Octave plus seventh

Table 3: The Initial Six Intervals Above the Octave

Compound intervals can have all the requirement of smaller intervals, which indicates a compound interval can be (contingent upon the interval) major, minor, great, augmented, or diminished.

Intervals and Half Steps

You may think about all these intervals as far as half-advances. To that end, the accompanying table shows the number of half advances between these major and minor intervals.

Half Steps Between Intervals

Interval	Number of Half Step
Perfect unison	0
Minor second	1
Major second	2
Minor third	3
Major third	4
Perfect fourth	5
Augmented fourth	6
Diminished fifth	6
Perfect fifth	7
Minor sixth	8
Major sixth	9

Table 4a: Half Step Advance between Intervals

Half Steps Between Intervals (continued)

Interval	Number of Half Steps
Minor seventh	10
Major seventh	11
Octave	12
Minor ninth	13
Major ninth	14
Minor tenth	15
Major tenth	16
Perfect eleventh	17
Augmented eleventh	18
Diminished twelfth	18
Perfect twelfth	19
Minor thirteenth	20
Major thirteenth	21
Minor fourteenth	22
Major fourteenth	23

Table 5(4b): Half Step Advance between Intervals

And take special consideration note of those intervals that are enharmonically identical—such as the augmented fourth and the diminished fifth. What you call that interval relies upon which bearing you're heading, and which notation is the easiest to read in a bit of music.

What You Need to Know

- When the least interval within any two notes is a half advance, the two half steps equal one entire advance.

- A sharp increase the value of a note by a half advance. A flat brings down the value of a note by a half advance.

- One portray the intervals between any two notes regarding degree. For instance, we refer the interval within the first and third notes to as a third.

- In a major scale, the seconds, thirds, sixths, and sevenths are referred to as major intervals. You can make a minor interval by flattening these notes.

- In a major scale, the fourths, fifths, and octaves are referred to as impeccable intervals.

- At the point when you flatten an ideal interval, you create a diminished interval; at the point when you sharpen an ideal interval, you create an augmented interval.

CHAPTER 03

SCALE

S cales are essential because you use them to create songs. You can create a pleasant-sounding song just by picking notes from a single major scale. For example, use the C Major scale (the white notes on a piano) and single out notes that sound great when played together. Make sure you start and end your song on the C note itself; you've recently composed a basic tune. Eight Notes Equal One A scale and is, basically, eight successive pitches inside a one-octave range. All scales begin on one note and end on that actual note, one octave higher. For example, each C scale starts on C and finishes on C; an F scale starts on F and finishes on F, and they all have six additional notes in the middle.

Fig 19: The Eight Notes of a Scale; C Major, Right Now.

We call the main note of a scale the tonic, or first degree of the scale. Not shockingly, we call the following note the subsequent degree, the third note is called an exhaustive round of questioning, and so on—until you get to the eighth note, which is the tonic. The major special case to the eight-note scale decides it is the scale that incorporates all the notes in an octave, including all the sharps and flats. We call this kind of scale a chromatic scale, and (when you start with C) looks something like this:

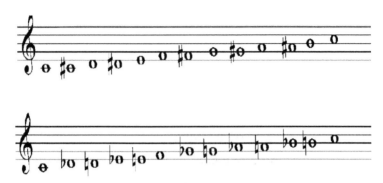

Fig 20: Chromatic Scale of a Music Starting with C

The **chromatic scale C**, the top staff explains the scale using sharps; the bottom staff shows the scale using flats. Any scale has specific relationships between the different degrees of the scale. That's how you can depict different scales. A major scale has different intervals between specific notes from those you'll discover on a similar minor scale. These different intervals give each sort of scale it's one of a kind of sound.

The most widely recognized scale is called the major scale. Major scales are delight scales; they have pleasant and expected intervals every step of the way. (Gently hum "Do Re Mi Fa So La Ti Do," and you'll hear this pleasant quality.) The perfect representation of the major scale is the minor scale. They say minor scales to be sad scales; the intervals between the notes sound a touch of discouraging. Either major or minor scales can begin on any note from A-flat down to G-sharp. No matter the exact note you start with, each scale has its specific combination of intervals between the notes. The accompanying areas broadly expound on both minor scales and major scale.

152

Major Scales

What comprise a major scale are the precise intervals between the notes of the scale. Each major scale uses the same intervals as shown on the accompanying table.

The Intervals of the Major Scale

Note	Half Steps to Next Note
Tonic	2
Second	2
Third	1
Fourth	2
Fifth	2
Sixth	2
Seventh	1

Table 6: The Same Interval of the Major Scale

In another form, the intervals in a major scale go this way: entire, entire, half, entire, entire, entire, half. If you start your major scale on C (the C Major scale), you wind up playing all white keys on the piano. C Major is the main major scale that uses just the white keys; all different scales have black keys in them. To make things easier for you, the accompanying table shows all the notes in the 15 major scales:

Minor Scales

Minor scales sound somewhat less "up" than major scales. This is mainly because the third note of the minor scale is a minor interval, meanwhile, the third note of the major scale is a major interval. That little half advance between a minor third and a major third makes all the difference on the planet! Not to confound you; however, whereas there was a single major scale, there are three sorts of minor scales: natural, harmonic, and melodic. We'll take a gander at each scale separately.

Natural Minor

The easiest minor scale to develop is the natural minor scale. You can consider the natural minor as far as its major comparing scale. At the point when you start and end a major scale on the 6th note, rather for the tonic, you get a natural minor scale. Here's an instance: Play a C Major scale (C D E F G A BC). Climb to the 6th note or descend two notes. (It's the same thing up to six or down to two; both put you on the A.) Now play an eight-note scale, but using the notes in C Major. What you make is **A B C D E F G** and is the minor (natural) scale. As you know, each natural minor scale receives the same tones as a specific major scale.

Relative Major and Minor Scales (continued)

Major Scale	Related Natural Minor Scale
F Major	D minor
F-sharp Major	D-sharp minor
G-flat Major	E-flat minor
G Major	E minor
A-flat Major	F minor
A Major	F-sharp (G-flat) minor
B-flat Major	G minor
B Major	G-sharp minor
C-flat Major	A-flat minor

Table 7: Relative Major and Minor Scale

In another form, the intervals in a natural minor scale go this way: entire, half, entire, entire, half, entire, entirety.

154

Harmonic Minor

We relate the harmonic minor scale to the natural minor scale, except for the seventh note which is raised a half advance. Some musicians favor this kind of minor scale because the seventh note better leads up to the tonic of the scale. The accompanying explains the intervals between the notes in the harmonic minor scale. The Intervals of the Harmonic Minor Scale are:

- Note Half Steps to Next Note
- Tonic 2
- Second 1
- Third 2
- Fourth 2
- Fifth 1
- Sixth 3
- Seventh 1

In another form, the intervals in a harmonic minor scale go this way: entirety, half, entire, entire, half, entire and a half, half.

Melodic Minor

The main issue with the harmonic minor scale is that the interval between the 6th and 7th notes are three half advances and you only, from time to time, have an interval in a scale more extensive than two half advances (It's simply too awkward even to consider singing.). So, the melodic minor scale increases both the 6th and seventh notes of the natural minor scale by a half advance each, subsequent in the accompanying intervals:

The Intervals of the Melodic Minor Scale

Note	Half Steps to Next Note
Tonic	2
Second	1
Third	2
Fourth	2
Fifth	♭2
Sixth	2
Seventh	1

Table 8: The Interval of the Melodic Minor Scale

In another form, the intervals in the melodic minor scale go this way: entirety, half, entire, entire, entire, entire, half.

As if three minor scales weren't sufficient to deal with, some music scholars use this melodic minor scale just when there is no a joke on the scale. (They refer to this as the ascending melodic minor scale.) Going back down (the sliding melodic minor scale), they use the notes in the natural minor scale. So, we raise the 6th and the 7th degrees in transit up, but not in transit down. Scholars are part of this issue; however, some uses the melodic minor scale, both ascending and slipping, and others use the two different scales. It's okay to use a single scale, as introduced here, where you're aware of the alternate way of getting things done. In the melodic minor scales and harmonic, the seventh degree is called the leading tone. In the melodic minor scale, the sixth degree is called the **submediant**. In the accompanying areas, we talk about the natural, harmonic, and melodic minor scales and how to play them on the piano and guitar.

156

Playing natural minor scales on guitar and piano

Natural minor scales reflect the interval pattern of WH-WWHWW, which translates into Whole advance Half advance Whole advance. The primary note (and last) in the scale decides the scale name. It produces a natural minor scale from the major scale of the related name, but with the third, sixth, and seventh degrees brought down by one-half advance. Along these lines, for instance, if someone asks you to play the scale for A-natural minor on the piano, you set it up as shown.

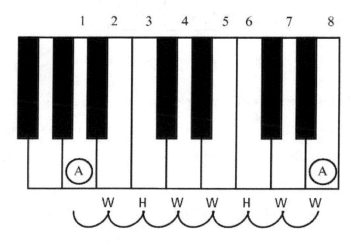

Fig 21: Setup of the A Natural Minor on Piano

Similarly, as with major scales, to play natural minor scales on the guitar, you have to move the figure shown below in pattern along the neck of the guitar to assemble whatever minor scale you'd prefer. Whatever note you start with on the apex (low E) string is the tonic, and consequently names the scale. If someone requests you to play an A minor scale on the guitar, for instance, you play the pattern shown below;

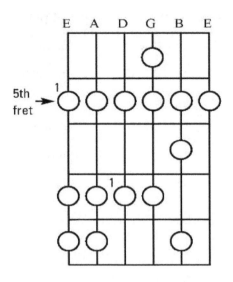

Fig 22: Setup of A minor Scale on Guitar

Having fun with harmonic minor scales on piano and guitar:

The harmonic minor scale is a variety of the natural minor scale (which we examined in the first area). It happens when a half-advance raises the seventh note of the natural minor scale. The progression isn't raised in the key signature; instead, it's raised using accidentals (sharps, twofold sharps, or naturals). This sometimes means that you will blend sharps and flats on the same scale, which is okay. To play A-harmonic minor A on the keyboard, you set up the scale as shown in Figure underneath.

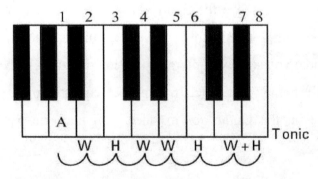

Fig 23: Setup of A-harmonic Minor A on the keyboard

At the point when you're composing music, and you want to use a harmonic scale, work it out using the natural minor key first, then return and add the accidental that raises the seventh degree a half advance. Playing harmonic minor scales on the keyboard is basic. You simply position the pattern shown in Figure below over the root (tonic) point that you want to play in. Move it around to a separate root to play the scale for that note.

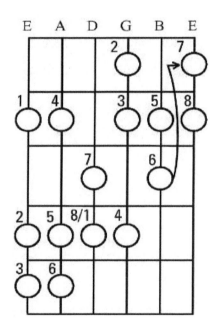

Fig24: Setup of Harmonic Minor Scale On the Keyboard

Producing great music with melodic minor scales on both piano and guitar:

We get the melodic minor scale from the natural minor scale. In these melodic minor scales, the 6th and 7th notes of the natural minor scale are both raised by one-half advance when going up the scale. However, remember that they come back to the natural minor when going down the scale. This scale is precarious, so we will reiterate: While you're going up in pitch when playing a piece, you raise the sixth and seventh degrees of the natural minor scale a half advance, but during parts of the same piece where the pitch moves down, you play the notes under the natural minor scale. Scales in which the sixth and seventh degrees are flat in natural minor will expect naturals to raise those two degrees.

Melodic minor scale arrangers work out the tune using the natural minor pattern, and then they add the accidentals that change any ascending sixth and seventh notes afterward. The superb thing about the guitar is that you just have to keep one pattern for each kind of scale, and you're set.

CHAPTER 04

WHAT IS A MODE?

t merits using the minor pentatonic scale to exhibit a significant idea. We saw that this scale comprises an assortment of 5 notes and that when they are arranged around the root, there is a specific arrangement of intervals that characterize the scale. However, imagine a scenario where we take those equivalent definite 5 notes for example, A minor. The pentatonic scale (A, C, D, E, and G) and **re-arrange them.** Imagine a situation in which as objected to calling A root; we treat this equivalent assortment of notes as a C scale, regarding C as the root. The notes have different names as:

- C is never again the minor third (of A); it is the Root.

- D is never again the Perfect fourth (of A), it is the Major second (of C),

- E is the Major third,

- G is the Perfect fifth, and,

- A is the Major sixth.

So, the new arrangement of notes is: **Root**, Major second, Major third, **Perfect fifth, Major sixth;** or: **R, M2, M3, P5, M6;** this is a different dynamic assortment of notes than the A-minor pentatonic scale, although it comprises a similar 5 tones because it is a different arrangement of intervals.

Major Pentatonic Structure

By using a similar example, yet starting at a different note, we have made a different scale. We know the scale that we have made as the **C major pentatonic scale,** and it's likewise a significant and fundamental scale in blues, nation, rock, pop, and so forth.

What we have made by re-situating the scale is known as a "**mode.** "We can say that the major pentatonic scale is a method of the minor pentatonic scale or that the minor pentatonic scale is a method of the major pentatonic scale (we, mostly, say the major pentatonic is gotten from the minor pentatonic because it is the mostly used one in all blues and rock). So, we get the major pentatonic scale from the minor pentatonic structure, just it starts on what was the second note of the minor pentatonic. Like the minor pentatonic scale, the major pentatonic scale is basic and conspicuous, and many of us know it without realizing it. Because of the different arrangement of intervals, this scale sounds different — it has a more beautiful, more joyful sound than its minor cousin, which is a consequence of the reality of it being a "major" scale.

The major pentatonic scale is, altogether, in the major scale, and so it is valuable at whatever point that scale can be used. Because there are 5 notes in the minor pentatonic scale, there are 5 different notes that can go about as the root of different modes. For each note in the assortment, there is a different mode where that note is the root, and we characterize the 4 different notes as for it, bringing about 5 different arrangements of intervals with each note. This is a fundamental understanding of modes. As your understanding and application in playing develop, you will begin considering them to be discrete scales as opposed to basic note re-directions of the parent scales (that is the reason you can once in a while use the terms 'scale' and 'mode' reciprocally).

On a more profound level, modes show the relationships among chords and scales, and they are comparative with the chords that are playing underneath, out of sight, or on the support track. This idea will be critical regarding 7-note scales, but first, we should handle the minor pentatonic scale modes.

Pentatonic Scale

The primary method of the minor pentatonic scale is only the minor pentatonic scale. It comprises a: Root, minor third, Perfect fourth, Perfect fifth, minor seventh. In A, the scale is: **A, C, D, E, G.** Here's the way this scale, or mode 1, sounds:

- Minor Pentatonic Scale Mode 1 sound model in A

- Minor Pentatonic Mode 2—Major

The second method of the minor pentatonic scale has an uncommon name. It is the major pentatonic scale, as we've found in the past area. It comprises the accompanying intervals: Root, Major second, major third, perfect fifth, major sixth

With shortened forms: R, M2, M3, P5, and M6 in C, the notes are: **C, D, E, G, A;** C is the relative major key of A-minor pentatonic, which is viewed as its parent scale. You don't have to understand this for the time being; but have the thought in your mind. Here is the key thing in the act of spontaneity portion for this mode we will play over A automaton note again so the tonal focus will be A. To hear how this mode sounds, we will play Major pentatonic scale, or mode 2 minor pentatonic scale, in An as opposed to C, over this sponsorship note. In my expectation, you're still with me. To do that, we need the notes of A-Major pentatonic scale, so we just apply the Major pentatonic equation beginning from A-note. However, here it is once more:

R =T =M2 = T = M3 = TS = P5 =T = M6 = TS = R

And the notes of the A Major pentatonic scale are:

A = T =B = T = C# = TS = E = T = F# = TS = An (Octave)

We should play these notes, advance a melody with them, and tune in to their personal impact over the An automaton note. This will give us the sound of the mode 2 of the minor pentatonic scale, or basically: Major pentatonic scale.

Minor Pentatonic Mode; sound model in A Once more, give close consideration to every note and how it sounds against the backing An automaton note; notice how the Major third, C# for this situation, gives it that major perky feel. Show restraint toward this.

Minor Pentatonic Mode 3; Envisaging your head doesn't hurt a lot after this, as we will look at another mode. Luckily, it's a similar idea

164

for different modes, and if you get it once, you get it for all modes. From that point, it's merely ceaseless practice and persistence. The third mode in our A minor pentatonic model starts on D and comprises a: Root, Major second, perfect fourth, Perfect fifth, minor seventh Or just: **R, M2, P4, P5, m7.**

We should rapidly recap how we got here (it's a similar procedure likewise with the Major pentatonic mode). In Mode 1 of the A minor pentatonic, the notes were: **A, C, D, E, G.** Mode 3 starts on the third note, which is D, and proceeds from that point. So the notes in D, will be **D, E, G, A, C. D** is never again Perfect fourth of A; it is the Root.

E is never again the Perfect fifth of A, it is the Major second comparative with D. G is never yet the minor seventh of A, it is the Perfect fourth relative to D. An is never again the Root, it is the Perfect fifth comparative with D, and C is never again the minor third of A, it is the minor seventh relative with D. Attempt to do this for modes 4 and 5 with no one else when we get to them; it will be a decent mental workout. Once more, D minor pentatonic mode 3 is a relative mode to the A minor pentatonic because and is liable for its characteristic sound.

Minor Pentatonic Mode 5

At long last, the fifth mode starts on the fifth note of the minor pentatonic scale, which in our A minor pentatonic model is G. It has a: Root, a Major second, a Perfect fourth, a Perfect fifth and a Major sixth Its notes, in G, will be: **G, A, C, D, E.** To get this current mode's sound over A automaton note used in the sound model, we should use minor pentatonic mode 5 out of A. Without rehashing the entire procedure, the notes of the fifth minor pentatonic mode in An, are:

$$A(R) = T = B(M2) = TS = D(P4) = T = E(P5) = T = F\#(M6) = TS\text{-}A\ A(O)$$

We've seen that mode 5 of A minor pentatonic is in G, with the notes: **G, A, C, D, E**. As it has been expressed a few times, the support ramble note in our sound impromptu creation passages is A, so to get the mode's sound, we needed to use minor pentatonic mode 5 out of A rather (it can get befuddling since methods of the minor pentatonic don't have exceptional names like the diatonic modes). The fact is, we could've used the fifth method of A minor pentatonic, which begins on G, for the act of spontaneity portions; however, all things considered, we would need to play over the G ramble.

Note to hear the qualities of the A minor pentatonic fifth mode sound. Since we played the fifth method of the minor pentatonic in A, would you be able to make sense of its parent minor pentatonic scale? Its B minor pentatonic. Don't be stressed if you don't get this now, it will be more apparent when we get to diatonic modes, recall, modes are comparative with what's playing in the foundation—playing something very similar over different support will have different impacts. On another note, the sound of a mode turns into more apparent when it's played over a full harmony or a harmony movement in the support track. Although it's significant (and simpler to learn modes) to begin with an automaton note and keep it straight toward the start, we can't seem to go over the chords later in the book.

166

Minor Pentatonic Mode Comparison Charts

To summarize, here's a table showing minor pentatonic modes in A with their interval capacities:

MODES	NOTES	1 R	2 m2	3 M2	4 m3	5 M3	6 P4	7 Aug 4th	8 P5	9 m6	10 M6	11 m7	12 M7	Octave
	1st mode (minor pentatonic scale)	A			C		D		E			G		A
	2nd mode (Major pentatopnic scale)	C		D		E			G		A			C
	3rd mode	D		E			G		A			C		D
	4th mode	E			G		A			C		D		E
	5th mode	G		A			C		D		E			G

Table 7: Minor pentatonic modes in A

If you need a decent workout, you can attempt to round out this table in a different key, for instance, C (you would begin with C as the root note in the upper left corner).

Minor Pentatonic Mode 1	R	m3	P4	P5	m7	Intervals
	1	b3	4	5	b7	Notes
Minor Pentatonic Mode 2 — Major Pentatonic Scale	R	M2	M3	P5	M6	Intervals
	1	2	3	5	6	Notes
Minor Pentatonic Mode 3	R	M2	P4	P5	m7	Intervals
	1	2	4	5	b7	Notes
Minor Pentatonic Mode 4	R	m3	P4	m6	m7	Intervals
	1	b3	4	b6	b7	Notes
Minor Pentatonic Mode 5	R	M2	P4	P5	M6	Intervals
	1	2	4	5	6	Notes

Table 8 Minor Pentatonic Interval Comparison

Notice in Table shown above how notes and their capacities change with different modes:

Notice, for instance, how modes 2 and 5 are comparable — Mode 2 has a Major third (3), and Mode 5 has Perfect fourth (4). Search for examples, and notice the differences. We will proceed to 7-note scales, on the whole.

What Does this Term "Diatonic" Mean?

A scale is diatonic when it is a mode, or variety, of the major scale. This incorporates the regular minor scale and each of the 7 of the diatonic methods (of which the major and minor scales are two). **"Diatonic"** is Greek, and it signifies "over the octave." The name alludes to how the structure of diatonic scales is with the end goal that there is even dissemination of 7 notes over the 12-note octave. There will never be, in any diatonic scale, over a full (entire) advance between two notes, and the half-steps are spread out by two complete advances. While there are 7 diatonic scales called the **diatonic modes**, which incorporates the major scale and the minor scale, there is just a single diatonic structure. This is because we characterize every of the 7 of those scales with each other. We produce them from each other (however, we regard them to be made from the major scale because it is the most key scale).

They share a structure because they are viably a similar 7-note design starting at different notes/focuses (if you treat the primary note of the major scale as the first note of the diatonic structure, at that point you can characterize a different scale climbing that structure yet starting on the subsequent note, or the fifth note, or some other note — only like the minor pentatonic modes).

Since there is just in certainty one diatonic structure, it is conceivable to speak both about diatonic scales (which means the methods of the major scale) and likewise about THE diatonic scale (as in the hidden structure

168

of those modes). This is a select utilization and understanding of the expression "diatonic scale," which isn't entirely predictable, yet is by a long shot the most widely recognized and suggested. A few scholars likewise incorporate harmonic and melodic minor modes as diatonic for specific reasons; however, this is a lot rarer and can cause some disarray.

7-Note Diatonic Scales; Norma Major and Natural Minor Scale

As we probably are aware now, the most essential, crucial sort of 7-note scale is known as a **"diatonic** scale." This class incorporates what are likely the two most effectively conspicuous scales by name: **the natural major scale** (normally substantially "the major scale") and the **normal minor scale** (basically "the minor scale"). These two scales structure the harmonic and melodic bedrock that Western music lies on and has laid on for a prolonged period. We find comparable scales since the commencement of world music (in customary Indian music, for example). It is significant now that, like with the minor pentatonic and major pentatonic, characteristic major and standard minor scales are mostly the methods of one another, however, with the major scale being thought of as the most key diatonic scale. Likewise, what's important is that the 5-note major pentatonic scale is much the same as the 7-note regular major scale, then actually two notes are overlooked. The same applies to minor pentatonic and the characteristic minor scale. These pentatonic scales originated from the longing to expel the intervals that are a semitone separated in the diatonic structure. For this reason, minor and major pentatonic scales are simplified and more secure, sounding minor and major scales.

Clarifying Diatonic Modes

If there is one thing that alarms musicians, specifically guitarists, it is the diatonic modes. Broadly known, yet once in a while comprehended, "the modes" are almost mythic for some players at many levels. Majority of us know that the modes are significant, that extraordinary players thoroughly understand them, however, it feels like they are miles away — some portion of what individuals call "music theory" and not in any manner what we can understand, substantially less make utilization. Perhaps we have known about modular jazz and accept that the modes are essential to propel jazz players with long periods of formal preparation, however, that they are something else pointless or past our span.

The modes are not gigantic. They are not a legend. They are not just for individuals who spend their 20s in music school. They aren't only for jazz musicians, and they aren't when you have learned them, any more difficult to use than any different scales. What they are, however, is significant. The modes give us an approach to understanding the relationship between different scales, offer us an assortment of scales to browse and give us the devices to make or extemporize over and in virtually any harmonic framework. We have seen that a mode is just a re-direction of a scale, treating a different note as the root and re-characterizing different notes in the scale. The notes remain the equivalent, however since the harmonic focus is different, the arrangement of intervals has changed (what was an ideal fifth in the A minor scale turns into a major third in the C major scale). And that is the pith of method the reality of the family member harmonic estimation of notes. A note is not a static, perpetual thing; a note does different things in different settings (contingent upon the harmony that is playing underneath or in the foundation). It is relative. That is how confounds many players, and it is the explanation that the modes are frequently evaded. Before going any further, it is essential to understand two terms; **Relative and parallel Modes, Parent Scales and Tonal Center.** When we talk about modes and scales, we talk around two different ways for scales to identify with each other consonantly. One is being in correspondence, and the other is being relative.

Relative Modes

Relative modes are what the most significant part many of us thinks about when we talk about "the modes," and it is how the modes have been introduced up to this point. Relative modes are scales that contain the entirety of similar notes yet start at separate positions. C major, A minor is also relative scales; the same applies to G major and E minor. Returning to the minor pentatonic modes, they said it that the entire methods of the minor pentatonic are relative to each other because they share the equivalent notes, as we've seen. **Relative modes** are helpful when expanding a piece up or down the harmonic space, for example, on a guitar fretboard. They are additionally valuable when making sense of which chords will substitute best for different chords, yet we'll get to that later in the book.

Parent scales

This is the scale that we get different modes from. As we've seen, for each of the 5 methods of the minor pentatonic, the primary mode — the minor pentatonic, is thought about the Parent minor scale, since we get different modes from it. It is essential to have the option to tell what the parent scale of every mode you experience is. For instance, would you be able to make sense of what is the parent scale of minor pentatonic mode 4 in **C#?** It's (**F#, A, B, C#, E**). So the minor parent scale of the minor pentatonic mode 4 **in C#, is F#** minor pentatonic. There are speedier strategies to make sense of the parent scales, which include using your instrument. However, this is something that will fall into place with time as you keep on using modes in your playing. On the guitar fretboard, for example, there are physical shapes you can get from the notes and their positions relative to each other, and you can picture this shape whenever you need to review the Parent scale and other relative methods of a mode rapidly.

Tonal focus

Tonal focus resembles the focal point of gravity—it is typically the harmony or a note (as in our case with sound models) that we play the mode over. At the point when we use a mode, there are a few notes that will help characterize the tonal focus in our performance. These are the **acceptable notes**, or you could likewise consider them the home notes. These notes are the notes of the harmony that is playing out of sight at the minute, and the most grounded of them is the Root note (it is usually the most secure one to land on during playing). At that instance, there are a few notes that pull away from the tonal focus, setting up development, and there are some that will include heaps of strain, which will be set out to a home note. There are likewise awful notes, which can genuinely conflict with the tonal focus or different notes playing out of sight, and they usually won't sound great by any means.

Parallel Modes

A parallel mode or scale is only a scale that offers its root with the first scale being alluded to. The modes that provide the comparable tonal center are parallel. For example, A major and A minor are parallel modes, B minor pentatonic and B major pentatonic are parallel modes, likewise E Locrian and E Lydian (don't worry over the luxurious names for the present), or some other mode/scale with a comparative starting note. In sound models for the minor pentatonic modes, we played parallel modes against the A robot note.

Relative modes share a similar parent scale

They have related notes, requested differently, yet they have different Roots, which imply they have different tonal focuses. Parallel modes then again share a similar root — the equivalent tonal focus, yet they have different Parent scale. This qualification is imperative to understand and recall.

Diatonic Modes Spelled Out

We can see that the major scale is a method of the minor scale and that the minor scale is a method of the major scale. When all is said and done, we take the major scale to be essential when discussing the diatonic modes. When we say **"the modes,"** we are often considering these scales diatonic scales: the major scale and its modes, which incorporate the standard minor scale. 7 notes are in the diatonic scale; likewise, there are 7 diatonic modes. Not at all like the diatonic modes, pentatonic scale modes, each has their very own Greek name, and those names are how we allude to the modes when we are thinking modularly. Once more, we will have sound models for every mode in a similar arrangement:

1. A scale/mode played here and there

2. Chords from that scale played all together (in a group of three structures)

3. An act of spontaneity portion, this time over the C ramble note.

The key we'll be using is C Major, and the entire ad-lib passages will be played over C ramble note.

Ionian Mode

The primary mode is the typical Major scale. We know this as the Ionian mode. The notes include **the following C, D, E, F, G, A, B in C,** It comprises a: Root, Major second, Major third, Perfect fourth, Perfect fifth, Major sixth, Major seventh. This mode has an upbeat, melodic, consonant sound. We have just inspected this scale/mode in the past segments. In the act of spontaneity selection, we will play this mode over C ramble note so we will use C Ionian mode, you could say normal C major scale.

Dorian Mode

The second method of the Major scale is the Dorian mode. It begins with the second note of the Major scale. The **Dorian** mode is minor (however, it isn't "the minor scale") since its third is minor and not major (this is how scales are partitioned among major and minor). The notes include the following **D, E, F, G, A, B, C in D.** It's Root, Major second, minor third, Perfect fourth, perfect fifth, Major sixth, minor seventh.

How could we get this interval, is simple only for this mode but how about we do a snappy recall. D Dorian applies to C Major Scale just because, as should be obvious, they share the equivalent notes yet have different tonal focuses. Since we all recognize the notes in C Major, we identify them in D Dorian too, and it's anything but difficult to make sense of the intervals from there:

- D is the Root

- E is the Major second-up from D.

- F is the minor third up from D.

- G is the Perfect fourth up from D.

- An is the Perfect fifth up from D

- B is the Major sixth up from D

- C is the minor seventh up from D

Another approach to get to this interval structure without the tonal focus is to take the major scale equation: **T S T S** — and re-situate it as we did with the notes. Since this mode begins the second note of the Major scale, we start on the second 'T' (bolded). So the scale equation for Dorian mode is **T S T S T.** we start from the Root (which could be any note) and proceed from there:

R – P4 =T = M2 = S = m3 = T = T = P5 = T = M6 = S = m7 =T = R (O).

The Dorian mode is darker compared to the Ionian mode because of the minor third, yet it sounds somewhat more brilliant than the minor scale because of the Major sixth. It is a normal scale in jazz and particularly blues. Try to counsel the Scale Correlation Charts a short time later to search for these differences. Like with the pentatonic modes, we will play this mode in parallel since our ramble note is C. That implies that we will play C Dorian mode over C in the extemporization passage.

First, we have to make sense of the notes in C Dorian, which is overly simple because we can apply its Dorian scale formula or its interval structure, the two of which we're comfortable with the following;

C = T = D = S =Eb = T = F = T =G = T = A = S = Bb = T = C (O)

Would you be able to clarify why we used b's writing out these notes and not #'s? Once more, tune in with the impact of each note over the automaton note. Notice which notes are steady and safe sounding and which ones are increasingly offensive giving strains, and how that pressure is discharged to a constant note.

Phrygian Mode

The third mode is the **Phrygian mode**. The third notes begin with the Major scale. It is a minor mode (the reason for the minor third), however again, it isn't the normal minor scale; its notes include the following **E, F, G, A, B, C, D in note E.** The minor second note is only a half-advance over the Root, so this note includes a great deal of discord because it normally needs to set out to the closest tonic (the

Root). This mode is used in some jazz metal, just as Latin and Indian impacted music.

In the sound mode, we use C Phrygian over the C ramble note. The notes in C Phrygian include the following,

C (R), =Db (m2), =Eb (m3), =F (P4) = G (P5) = Ab (m6) = Bb (m7)

Lydian Mode

The fourth mode is the Lydian mode. It begins the fourth note of the Major scale. This is a major scale because its third is major, and its notes in F will be: **F, G, A, B, C, D, E.** it has a: Root, Major second, Major third, Augmented fourth (Tritone), Perfect fifth, Major sixth, Major seventh The Lydian mode is a delightful sounding mode — like the major scale (it differs from it just by one note: the Tritone), just somewhat progressively intriguing. There is an unobtrusive cacophony in this mode; however, it is a major mode, and so it will sound rather perplexing, even sophisticated. We commonly use it in jazz instead of a major scale and over specific jazz chords. In as much C Lydian mode is to play above the C meander aimlessly note, we'll need the notes of the C Lydian scale: **C (R) = D (M2) =E (M3) = F# (Aug4) =G (P5) = A (M6) = B (M7)**

Mixolydian Mode

The fifth mode is the Mixolydian mode. It starts on the fifth note of the Major scale. They are major mode, and its notes in G can't avoid being: **G, A, B, C, D, E, F.** It includes Root, Major 2nd, and Major 3rd and Perfect 4th and Perfect 5th and Major 6th and minor 7th. The Mixolydian mode is a phenomenal blues scale and has a round, stable sound. Like with the Lydian mode, the principal difference to the Major scale is one note the minor seventh. In the sound model, we will use C Mixolydian to play over a C note. Its notes include: **C (R) = D (M2) = E (M3) = F (P4) =G (P5) = A (M6) = Bb (m7)**

Aeolian Mode

The 6th mode is the Aeolian mode. This is the Natural minor scale. In A, its notes include **A, B, C, D, E, F, G.** It has a: Root, Major second, minor third, Perfect fourth, Perfect fifth, minor sixth, minor seventh. The Aeolian mode is very dim, even dismal sounding; however, it isn't conflicting, and we use it generally used in, practically, a wide range of music. We have analyzed this scale in the minor scale area. In the natural creation extract, we will use C Aeolian mode or C Natural minor scale. Its notes are:

C (R) = D (M2) = Eb (m3) = F (P4)= G (P5) = Ab (m6) = Bb (m7)

Locrian Mode

The seventh and the last mode is the Locrian mode. It begins the seventh note of the Major scale. On account of C Major, it begins on B; so in B, its notes are **B, C, D, E, F, G, A.**

It contains a: Root, minor second, minor third, Perfect fourth, reduced fifth (Tritone), minor sixth, minor seventh; this mode is peculiar and seldom used it is a minor scale, yet the two its second and fifth notes are flat; it is the main diatonic mode without a Perfect fifth; the **Locrian** mode in this way is exceptionally flimsy. Usually, this scale was stayed away from inside and out. Its sound is overwhelming, conflicting, and rickety. We'll be using C Locrian in the act of spontaneity selection over the C ramble note. The notes in C Locrian include:

C (R) = Db (m2) = Eb (m3) =F (P4) = Gb (dim5) = Ab (m6) = Bb (m7)

CHAPTER 05

MAJOR AND MINOR KEYS

t is easy if you're creating music inside the C Major scale. All the notes fall in the space and lines of the treble, bass and clefs; no sharps or flats are necessary. (And, if you're playing the organ, you don't have to use those questionable black keys!) However, if you're creating music using another scale, use accidentals to raise and lower notes past the white keys on the piano keyboard. For instance, if you're using the F Major scale, you have a bothersome B-flat to deal with. By and by, you could place a flat sign before each B-flat in your music. However, you'll wind up making a lot out of flats, which is a major pain in the butt. Fortunately, there's an easy way to designate predictable flats and sharps throughout a whole bit of music, without noting every instance.

Key to Success

When a bit of music is based on a particular musical scale, we say that music is in the "key" of that scale. For example, a tune based around the C Major scale is in the key of C Major. A tune based around the B-flat Major scale is in the key of B-flat Major. When you assign a key to a bit of music (or to an area inside a larger part), it's assumed that the greater part of the notes in that music will stay inside the comparing scale. Therefore, if a song is written in A Major, most of the notes in the tune and harmonies should be inside the A Major scale.

Using Key Signatures

A helpful aspect concerning assigning a particular key to a bit of music is that it enables you to designate the sharps and flats upfront, without having to repeat them each time they happen in the music. Here's how its capacities.

You designate a key by embedding a key signature at the very beginning of the music, besides the primary clef on the principal staff. This key signature shows the sharps and flats used in that certain key. At that point, when you play through the whole piece, you automatically sharpen and flatten the correct notes. For example, suppose you composed a tune around the F Major scale. The F Major scale, if you can remember, has one flatted note: B-flat. So, besides the principal clef on the first staff, you put a flat sign on the B line. By and by, when you play that tune, each time you see a B, you play B-flat.

Fig 25: Key Signature

The key signature concerning the key of F, note the flat sign on the B line, showing the automatic B-flat. The same would happen if you were playing in the key of G, which contains one sharp: **F-sharp**. You set a sharp sign on the top F line on the first staff; at that point, each time you see an F, you play an **F-sharp**.

Major Keys

Similarly, as there are 15 major scales (checking three enharmonic), there are 15 major keys, each with its key signature.

Minor Keys

The key signatures applied to show major keys also can speak to the natural minor keys. As you recall from the previous Chapter, we base a natural minor scale on the same notes as a major scale but starts on the sixth note of the scale. This same technique applies to keys, so that (for example) the key of A minor uses the same notes—and the same key signature—as C major.

Understanding the Circle of Fifths

In the 6th century B.C., the Greek scholar and philosopher Pythagoras attempted to make things easier for everyone by standardizing or possibly dissecting musical tuning. He had already discovered the relationship between pitch frequencies and lengths of string and had defined what an octave was, so he figured standardizing tuning was the next logical step. He divided a circle into 12 equal sections, like a clock. The result of his experimentation eventually became known as the Circle of Fifths, which is as yet used today. Each of the 12 focuses around the circle was assigned a pitch value, which relates to the current system of an octave with 12 half advances. Western music scholars have since updated Pythagoras' Circle of Fifths to what you find in Figure beneath. There's a fast way to recall how many sharps or flats to incorporate with each key signature. We call this strategy the hover of fifth; it works this way. Starting with the key of C, for each ideal fifth you climb, you add a sharp. So, the **key of G** (an ideal fifth up from C) has one sharp. The **key of D** (an ideal fifth up from G) has two sharps and so on. The hover of fifths works the other way for flats. For each ideal fifth, you descend from C; you add a flat. So the key of F (an ideal fifth down from C) has one flat. The key of B-flat (an ideal fifth down from F) has two flats and so on. The accompanying drawing shows how all the major keys relate to the hover of fifths. At the point when you move clockwise around the circle, you're moving through the fifths (and the sharp keys); when you move counterclockwise, you're moving down through the fifths (and the flat keys).

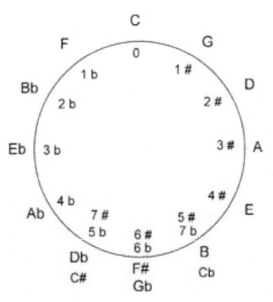

Fig26: Circle of Fifths

All the major keys are a fifth apart in the hover of fifths.

The following Figure shows the hover of fifths for the 15 minor keys. It works exactly the same as the major-key circle; move clockwise for the sharp keys, and counterclockwise for the flat keys.

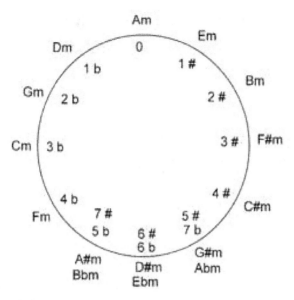

Fig27: The Circle of Fifths Works for Minor Keys.

Accidents Will Happen

When you dedicate a key signature to a piece of music, it's expected that all the following notes will correspond to that key. How do you show notes that fall outside that key? It ought to be noted that you can play outside a key. For instance, it's okay to play the special B natural when you're in the key of F, which normally has a B-flat. Nobody will arrest you for it. In fact, certain types of music regularly use non-scale notes.

When you conclude to write a note that isn't inside the current key, you have to manually show the change in the music—by utilizing sharp, flat, or natural signs. When musicians see the imputed flat, sharp, or natural, they know how to play the note as written, alternatively as showed by the music's key signature. Those "outside the key" notes are named accidentals or chromatic notes; they're normal. For instance, let's say a piece of music is in the key of F, which has just a single flat (B-flat).

185

You want your song to include an E-flat, which isn't part of the key. So when you approach that note, you input a flat sign before the E to show an E-flat. It's as simple as that.

Fig 28: Use Accidentals to Indicate notes Outside the Current Key Signature.

Accidents Will Happen

When you dedicate a key signature to a piece of music, it's expected that all the following notes will correspond to that key. How do you show notes that fall outside that key? It ought to be noted that you can play outside a key. For instance, it's okay to play the special B natural when you're in the key of F, which normally has a B-flat. Nobody will arrest you for it. In fact, certain types of music regularly use non-scale notes.

When you conclude to write a note that isn't inside the current key, you have to manually indicate the change in the music—by using sharp, flat, or natural signs. When musicians see the imputed flat, sharp, or natural, they know how to play the note as written, alternatively as showed by the music's key signature. Those "outside the key" notes are named accidentals or chromatic notes; they're normal. For instance, let's say a piece of music is in the key of F, which has just a single flat (B-flat). You want your song to include an E-flat, which isn't part of the key. So, when you approach that note, you input a flat sign before the E to show an E-flat.

186

Note that the accidental isn't applicable to any other notes in the second measure. It applies just to the tied note.

Fig 29 Accidentals Apply to all Notes tied Over a Measure.

If you figure other musicians, you may be confused about whether a note has reverted to normal, it's okay to use courtesy, sharp, flat, or natural sign. (This is a sign placed inside parentheses)s

Fig: 30 A courtesy Accidental Reminds Musicians that a Changed Note has Reverted to Normal.

Changing Keys

Some extended pieces of music don't usually use the same key all through the entire piece. Some short pop tunes change keys midway through. It's permitted. When a key is changed in the middle of a tune, it's called **modulating** to another key. Any key can be modulated, although the most widely recognized modulations are up a half step (from E Major to F Major, for example), or a fourth or fifth (from E Major to either A Major or B Major, for instance). When you want to change keys, you show this by inserting a new key signature in the primary measure of the new key. It's as easy as that, as you can see in the accompanying Figure. (Note that some composers and arrangers also input a double bar whenever there's a key change.)

Fig 31: To change keys, insert a new key signature.

The main complicated key change is when you're changing to the key of C, which has no sharps or flats. You indicate this by using natural signs to cancel out the previous sharps or flats, like this:

Fig 32: How to change to the key of C.

The things you Need to Know;

- You use key signatures to show what scale your music is particular on.

- To show notes outside the present key, use accidentals sharps, flats, and natural signs.

- In other to change the key in the middle of a piece of music, insert a new key signature.

- The flats sharps in a key signature are applied automatically all through the entire tune

- the key in the middle of a piece of music, insert a new key signature

CHAPTER 06

INTRODUCING TIME SIGNATURES

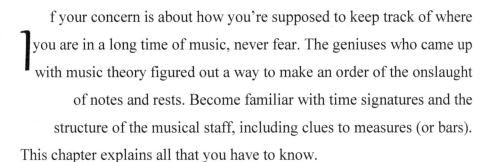

f your concern is about how you're supposed to keep track of where you are in a long time of music, never fear. The geniuses who came up with music theory figured out a way to make an order of the onslaught of notes and rests. Become familiar with time signatures and the structure of the musical staff, including clues to measures (or bars). This chapter explains all that you have to know.

Disentangling the Time Signature and Measures

In printed music, directly after the clef and the key signature (see Chapter 8 about key signatures) at the start of the staff, you see a pair of numbers, one composed over the other. The pair of numbers refers to the time signature, which, naturally, is the main subject of this chapter. The time signature discloses to both of your things: The number of beats in each measure: The top number in the time signature discloses to you the number of beats to be made a note of in each measure. If the number above is three, each measure comprises three beats. Which note gets one beat: The base number in the time signature reveals to you which sort of note value equals one beat — regular, eighth notes, and quarter notes. If the base number is four, a quarter notes is a beat. If the number eight, an eighth note carries the beat. The Figure beneath shows three regular time signatures.

Fig 33: Composed music contains the accompanying two main sorts of time
signatures, which we spread later right now

▶ **Straightforward:** With basic time signatures, we can separate
the beat off a bit of music into two-part rhythms.

▶ **Compound:** In the compound time signatures, the beat is
brother down into three-part rhythms. A measure (sometimes
referred to as a bar) is a section of composed music contained
inside two vertical lines. Each measure in a bit of music has as
many beats as is allowed during signature. In cases, if you're
working with a 4/4-time signature, each measure in that bit of
music will contain exactly four beats carried by notes on rests. If
the time signature is 3/4, both measures will have three beats in
it. The one special case to this standard is the point at which the
measure uses get notes. With these notes, you can put a strong
sting on the main beat of each measure, the "1" beat. Musicians
call this the downbeat.

▶ **Figure beneath:** Given the 3/4-time signature, each measure
contains three beats, and the quarter note equals one beat.

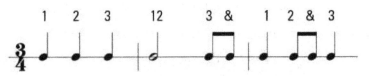

Fig 34: Three Bits and Quarter note

Practicing tallying through measures is a great way to make sure you're playing the bit of music before you according to the beat picked by the arranger. As we make clear in past Chapters, consistently including beats in your head while you're playing is unbelievably important to the subsequent sound. Timing is everything in music. You should be so comfortable with the inalienable beat of whatever you're playing that you don't realize you're checking beats anymore.

Keeping It Simple with Simple Time Signatures

Basic time signatures are the easiest to check because a one-two heartbeat in a bit of music feels the most natural to an audience and an entertainer. The accompanying four necessities show that a period signature is straightforward:

We isolate each beat into two equal segments

If a solitary beat has over one note, we always group those notes into one equal beat. This characteristic is most clear when it's applied to eighth and smaller notes. In basic time, two eighth notes are always associated together with a bar called a beam, as are four sixteenth notes, or eight thirty-second notes. (If you have two sixteenth notes and one-eighth note, those three notes, which equal one beat, are also beamed together.) The Figure below shows the movement of how notes are beamed together in basic time.

Figure beneath

Each degree of this tree equals each other layer, and different notes inside a beat are always grouped to equal one beat.

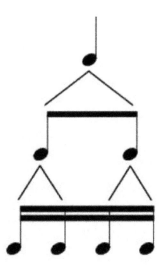

Fig 35: The Note that Makes One Beat has to be Undotted.

When you're excluding a tune in your head, you're just going to check undotted notes detachable by two. Usually, this means you'll be checking quarter notes, but you also may tally half notes, entire notes, or, most times, eighth notes. In 4/4 time, for instance, in your head, you'll be checking, "One-two-three-four" again and again. In 3/4 time, it'll be "one-two-three" again and again; in 2/4 time, "one-two." The top number isn't separable by three except for when it is 3. For instance, 3/4 and 3/8 are viewed as basic time signatures, whereas 6/4, 6/8, and 9/16 aren't (because they are separable by 3; we refer them to as compound time signatures).

The figure of beats is the same in each measure

Each measure, or bar, of music in a basic time signature has the same number of beats throughout the tune. After you get into the score of checking out the time, you don't have to stress over-busy, but making sure the notes in tune follow that beat all the way through. Using measures to include in straightforward time Measures (or bars), assist entertainers with monitoring where they are in a bit of music and assist them with playing the correct beat. In a straightforward time, the measure is the place the genuine musicality of a bit of music can be felt, regardless of whether you're reading a bit of sheet music without playing it. And remember that in basic time, we place a somewhat stronger accent on the principal beat of each measure. Here are some basic examples of straightforward time signatures:

- 4/4: Used in classical, rock, popular, jazz, nation, blue-grass, hip-jump, and house music

- 3/4: Used for waltzes and nation and western ballads

- 2/4: Used in polkas and marches

- 3/8: Used in waltzes, minuets, and nation and western ballads

- 2/2: Used in marches and moderate moving processionals

Counting 4/4 time

When a line of music has 4/4-time signature like the one in Figure beneath, the beat is numbered this way: ONE TWO THREE FOUR. A period signature of 4/4 satisfies the prerequisites of straightforward time.

Fig 36: Counting 4/4 time

The base number 4 in the time signature in Figure 4-4 reveals to you that the quarter note gets the beat, and the top number 4 discloses to you that each measure contains four beats or four quarter notes. Because 4/4 time is so regularly used in popular sorts of music, it's as often as possible alluded to as basic time. In fact, instead of stating "4/4" for the time signature, some authors compose a large "C" instead of Checking 3/4 time If the time signature of a line of music is 3/4, as in Figure underneath, the beat tallied this way: ONE two three. A period signature of 3/4 satisfies the necessities of the straightforward time.

Fig 37: Counting 3/4 time

Checking 3/8 time if the time signature is 3/8, the principal note — whatever it maybe — gets the beat. The Figure showed that the first note is an eighth note. Figure underneath: A period signature of 3/8 satisfies the necessities of the straightforward time.

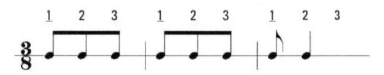

Fig 38: Counting 3/8 time

You need to count out the beat of the music shown in Figure above like this: ONE two three. The time signatures 3/8 also 3/4 have almost the same cadence structure in the way we make the beat a note of.

Therefore, because 3/8 uses eighth notes instead of a quarter notes, the eighth notes get the beat. Counting the beat 2/2 time; If the time signature of a line is 2by2, also referred to cut time, the half note gets the beat. And because the top number discourages mines that the measure contains two beats, you realize that each measure has two half notes, as shown in Figure underneath. Figure beneath: In 2/2 time, the half note gets the beat, and each measure contains two beats.

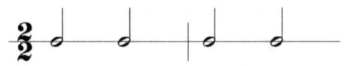

Fig 39: You include the music in Figure above like this: ONE two ONE two

Time signatures with a two as the lower number were generally used in medieval and pre-medieval music. Music from this period used a mood structure, called a tactus, later called a minim that was based on the musicality pattern of a human heartbeat. Practicing including beats in basic time using the information from earlier in the chapter, practice checking out the beats (not the notes) shown in Figures. When forgetting about these beats boisterous, give the primary beat a slight pressure. For a challenge, give tapping a shot on the notes while you forget about the beats uproarious.

Working with Compound Time Signatures

Just a little bit trickier than directly, time signatures are compound signatures. Here's a short rundown of decisions that help you immediately tell when you're dealing with a compound time signature: The top number is uniformly distinct by 3, except for time signatures in which the top number is 3. Signature with a top number of

6, 9, 12, 15, and so on according to the products of 3 is a compound time signature. But, 3/4 and 3/8 aren't compound time signatures because the top number is 3 (they're basic time signatures, which I examine earlier). The most widely recognized compound time signatures are 6/8, 9/8, and 12/8.

Using measures to include in compound time, One major difference between music in a basic time signature and music in compound time signature is that they feel different, both to tune in to and to play. In compound time, an accent isn't just placed on the principal beat of each measure (as in straightforward time), but we also place a marginally gentler accent is also on each successive beat. Hence, there are two particularly accented beats in each measure of music with a 6/8 time, three accents in a bit of 9/8 music, and four accents in a bit of music with a 12/8-time signature. Some examples of compound time signatures are 6/8: Used in mariachi music 12/8: Found in 12-bar blues and doo-wop music 9/4: Used in jazz and dynamic stone.

Tip: To decide the number of accents per measure under a compound time signature, separate the top number by three. Doing so encourages you to discover the beat in the music you're playing and, along these lines, where to put the accents. In a bit of 6/8 music, for example, you would put the ac-penny at the start of each measure, but you also would put a slight accent at the start of the second group of eighth notes in a measure.

Counting 6/8 time the beat accents in Figure 4-15 would go this way: ONE two three FOUR five six ONE two three FOUR five six Right now,/8 time signature, you accent the first and the second arrangements of three eighth notes.

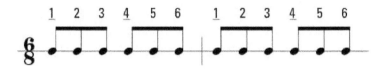

Fig 40: Counting 6/8

Counting 9/4 time; Peradventure the time signature is something scary, similar to 9/4, as shown in the example Figure above. You will count off the beat like so: ONE two three FOUR five six SEVEN eight nine.

Feeling the Pulse of Asymmetrical Time Signatures

Asymmetrical time signatures (also sometimes called mind-boggling or irregular time signatures) contain five or seven beats, compared to the traditional two-, three-, and four-beat measure groupings presented earlier right now. Asymmetrical time signatures are basic in traditional music from around the world, remembering for European people's music and in Eastern (particularly Indian) popular and society music. At the point when you play or hear a bit of music with an asymmetrical time signature, you notice that the beat of the tune feels and sounds a considerable amount different from music composed under basic or compound time signatures. Most Music with 5/4, 5/8, and 5/16-time signatures are usually separated into two heartbeats — either two beats besides three beats, or the other way around. The pressure pattern doesn't have to repeat itself from measure to measure; the main constant is that each measure despite everything contains five beats.

Playing with Beat

The standards of notes and rests may appear to be severe. Still, even the most casual audience can perceive that music isn't a power-constrained by automated percussionists and gigantic clicking metronomes. If the world itself were an impeccably requested organism, with each living thing on it moving along in immaculate time, all music might sound related. However, even the perfect healthiest human heart skips a beat once in a while, so does music. The stunt for authors and music scholars alike has being to translate these skipped beats into composed notation, making such deviations fit naturally into the score. This chapter explains all that you have to think about working with a beat.

Creating Stress Patterns and Syncopation

The basic cadenced beat of the music is called the beat. In some ways, the beat is everything. It decides how individuals dance to music or even how they feel when they hear it. The beat impacts whether individuals feel energized, agitated, smooth, or relaxed by music. At the point when you're recording a bit of music on paper, the way you group your notes in a measure (the music contained inside two bar lines) mirrors the beat the music will produce. As a musician, you can explore this natural heartbeat when you play music and count off the beats. Examining the general standard of placing pressure on the main beat of a measure gets the strongest pressure. If multiple beats are in a measure, usually, a strong secondary beat comes halfway through the measure. Lots of speculations exist about why the brain appears to demand that music be separated into units of two and three beats (not the least being that the beat of the music will be like the beat of the human heart). But nobody has gone to an agreement on why music ought to be divided into units of a few beats. In a bit of music with four beats in each measure, for example, a piece in 4/4 time, the main beat in the measure has a strong accent, and the third beat has a marginally less strong accent. Count the beats as complies: ONE two THREE four A bit of music written in 6/8 time, which has six beats in each measure, is counted: ONE two three FOUR five-six.

Syncopation: Hitting the strange

Syncopation is, essentially, a deliberate disturbance of the few beat pressure pattern. Musicians frequently create syncopation by focusing on a strange, or a note that isn't on the beat. In 4/4 time, the general pressure pattern is that the first and the third beats are strong, and the 2nd and 4th are weak. Another way to interpret this is that downbeats, or accented beats, for example, those at the start or halfway through a measure, are strong, and upbeats, or unaccented beats, are weak. So, if you had a bit of music that resembled the music, you view the quarter rest where the natural downbeat is located as the purpose of syncopation in the music. We stress the 4th beat of the measure instead of the third beat which is normally accented, creating a different-sounding mood than you would normally have in 4/4-time music. We would count the measure off as One-two-three-FOUR.

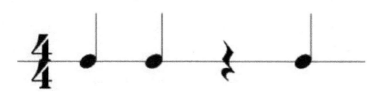

Fig 41: A measure with syncopation.

199

In the Figure, something has upset the natural apprehension of the meter. The count One-two- (three)- FOUR is peculiar to your ear because you want to hear that nonexistent quarter note that would carry the downbeat in the measure. If you do anything that upsets the natural beat with either an accent or an upbeat with no consequent down-beat being played, you have created syncopation. Individuals frequently mistake syncopation as being contained cool, complex rhythms with lots of sixteenth notes and eighth notes, as regularly heard in jazz music, but that isn't necessarily valid. For example, Figure beneath shows a lot of eighth notes and then a lot of sixteenth and thirty-second notes.

Fig 42: 6/8 Eighth Notes and then a lot of Sixteenth and Thirty-Second Notes

Because the Figure above shows a thick beat, it doesn't mean it syncopates thus rhythms. As you can understand from the accent marks, the downbeat is still on the "one" and "four" count in the two measures, which is the normal downbeat. Regardless of whether a bit of music contains a whole measure of eighth notes, it doesn't necessarily have syncopation. Each eighth note has a resulting cadenced goal. The downbeats despite everything happening are in the measure where they should be on the accented notes shown in the Figure. The same is valid for a lot of sixteenth notes in succession. They aren't syncopated because, again, although you have some intriguing notes that aren't on the downbeat, everything winds up always set out to the beat of ONE two THREE four, or ONE two three FOUR five-six. Inside each crate is a state of syncopation in the measures, giving you a cadence of knockout punch three FOUR one TWO three FOUR. A natural burden has been shifted over in the two measures, bringing about an intentionally disconnected sounding beat.

Figure underneath: This music shows two places where the note placement creates syncopation

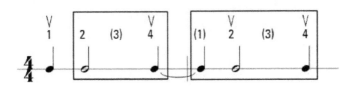

Fig 43: Two Places where the Note Placement Creates Syncopation

So, does syncopation include a carefully placed rest or an accented note? The answer is both. If your viewpoint of where the downbeat happens is moved, a state of syncopation results because it's shifting where the strong and the weak accents are fabricated.

Tip: Try counting out the beats while tuning in to the Rolling Stones' "Satisfaction," and you'll hear some great examples of syncopation.

Getting a Jump on Pick-Up Notes

As of recently, you've had to adhere to the standard that says 4/4 meter has four beats to each measure. Think about each measure like a container of water that you have to fill to fill up without overflowing; you can't wind up short, and you can't spill any finished. That's the standard. But like each great standard, this one has a special case. It's called a get measure, which is an odd measure at the start of a bit of music, as shown in Figure beneath. This measure contains notes as shown below;

Fig 44: 3/4 Counting Pick-Up Notes

The get measure shown in Figure 5-4 has just one beat where three ought to be (given that the piece is in 3/4 time). Starting there on, the melody adheres to the guidelines set out by the 3/4 time signature to the end.

The final measure is the 2nd part of the get measure: We view the final two beats as the remaining part of the primary measure. The last measure "fixes" what looked amiss with that first measure, and in this way, you have a bit of music composed according to all the standards of music hypothesis. Like a lot of instances when dealing with music hypothesis, the matter of using "get notes" is, mostly, notational. In contemporary music, especially exciting music, you can even now have the main get measure. Still, you don't have to adhere to the ideal principle of completing it in the final measure. Regularly musicians start a melody with a get measure, but they finish their last measure.

Irregular Rhythms: Triplets and Duplets

Another way you can add cadenced intrigue and variety to music is by using irregular rhythms (also called an irrational beat or artificial division). An irregular mood is any cadence that includes separating the beat differently based on what's allowed when signature. We call it the triplet; which are three notes combined that equate the beat of a solitary note. The second most basic kind of irregular cadence is a duplet which is two bracketed notes with a note value of three of the same notes.

Irregular note divisions, for example, triplets and duplets, allow for more mind-boggling rhythms than "regular" notation time normally allows.

Adding Enthusiasm with Triplets

Say you want to put a fast-little grouping of three notes where you'd normally play a one-quarter note. In 4/4 time, if you desire to play much number of notes in your grouping, you can use two or three eighth notes, or four sixteenth notes, or eight thirty-second notes. However, if you want to play an odd number of notes, and you want that odd number of notes to amount to one beat. The response is to play a triplet which is what you get when you have a note that's usually distinguishable by two equal parts partitioned into three equal parts.

Tip: A great way to count out the beats while playing triplets is to say the number of the beat followed by the word triplet (with two syllables), isolating the triplet played into three equal parts.

Working with Duplets works like triplets, aside from around. Authors use duplets when they want to place two notes in a space where they should put three. An example would partition a specked quarter note into two eighth notes instead of three eighth notes as you would in a measure of music under a compound time signature. A decent way to count duplets is to count the second note in each pair as and instead of assigning it a number value as you would any other beat in compound meter.

CHAPTER 07

MASTER THE CHORDS

What is a Chord?

Some instruments are single-note instruments, prepared to do just playing one note at once. Different instruments, however, similar to guitars and pianos, are ready to do playing of chords.

A harmony, at its essential, is just a music unit comprising multiple notes being played simultaneously. It is the sound we get when we merge any (at least two) notes and play them simultaneously. Chords originate from scales. They are from notes on a scale. Each scale suggests a specific rundown of chords; when you have a scale as the main priority, it is anything but difficult to produce chords that are contained in that scale; we'll get to this soon.

Chords are like scales, characterized by a lot of intervals relative to the root note. This is how we name the chords — the name of a harmony mentions to us what sort of notes it contains; it mentions to us what is the root note (could be any of the 12 notes), and from which we make the intervals harmony. The intervallic structure of harmony — the way the notes in harmony relate to its root note — is known as the "**spelling**" of that harmony, and if you know the name of the harmony, then you know, because of its spelling, the notes that are contained in it.

If we have a Major seventh harmony, for example, at that point before the finish of this chapter, you will figure out how it comprises some Root, a Major third, a Perfect fifth, and a Major seventh note (all relative to the root). This is the spelling of a Major seventh harmony. If we appoint this harmony a specific root note, for instance, G note, at that point the name of this harmony would be: G Major seventh; and if we at that point take a gander at the G major scale, we would realize that different notes in harmony, because of its spelling, are:

G(R)B(M3) D(P5)F# (M7)

It is conceivable, just by naming the intervals in harmony, to make exceptionally unpredictable chords (for example, a **Major 13 flat 9** harmony). These chords are most regularly used in jazz, and they make multiple harmonic spaces. Their utilization is exceptionally particular, with specific chords just being played in certain circumstances.

Chords Building

We work chords from intervals of thirds. They comprise a root note and another note, or arrangement of notes over that root that climb in thirds. To accomplish such a structure all, that is required is to take a scale and tally up from a root note by a third (which means up two degrees in the scale) to get a harmony note, and then for each new note in the harmony check-up by another third (to the fifth, the seventh, and so on). Thus, two scales, chords can be depicted by their harmony formulas. Since we make chords from notes of the scale they originate from, their formula shows the scale degrees that that harmony uses from its scale. If we have a "1 3 5 7" harmony formula, for instance (which is the formula for a Major seventh harmony), it implies that this harmony comprises the Root (first scale degree), third, fifth, and 7th scale degree. If we take a Major scale and dole it out a key, suppose key of C, we can apply this formula to get the notes of the C Major seventh harmony.

C	D	E	F	G	A	B
1	2	3	4	5	6	7

Table 9: The Formula

This is the reason **C** major seventh harmony comprises the notes: **C** (Root — give the harmony with its name), E (Major third), G (Perfect fifth), and **B** (Major seventh). Harmony formulas and harmony spelling are the same as and helpful ideas that give us a method for dissecting the chords. We'll investigate this significantly more in further areas.

It is conceivable, and reasonable, to change chords that have been worked by stacking thirds — by moving at least one note up or down, by altering the chords (revamping their notes) with the goal that another harmony is created, or by including a note from the scale you're working with to a previous harmony. It is moreover conceivable to make chords by stacking intervals other than thirds — for example, fourths or fifths, although this is far less normal. However, chords are created in the manner we have portrayed — by stacking thirds over a root note as per a specific scale.

Harmony Types (Dyads, Triads, Quadads) and Chord Qualities

A harmony is any sound created by more than one note. That implies that whenever at least two notes are created simultaneously, we frame harmony. We sort chords according to the number of notes in them, and although it is conceivable to discuss chords containing a lot of notes (up to twelve), the typical formulations contain two, three, or four notes. In jazz and some traditional chords with multiple notes happen with some frequency; however, when all is said and done, they are viewed as augmentations of three or four-note chords.

Regularly, chords comprise 3 or 4 particular notes, albeit commonly when we play a harmony, you can a rehash a portion of these notes in different octaves coming about in over 3 or 4 tones creating the harmony. This is self-evident, for instance, if you play a fundamental harmony on guitar, most novices initially adapt, for example, E minor, and at that point break down which notes you played — although you played each of the six strings, which implies six notes, there are just 3 particular notes in this harmony, some of which are rehashed on specific strings to get a full sounding harmony. The most widely recognized chords comprise basic 3-note chords, called groups of three. In progressively complex harmonies, most chords contain 4 notes (we know these as the seventh chords or quads).

We order most regular Harmony:

1. **Dyads**; these are chords containing any two notes.

2. **Groups of three**; these are chords containing three particular notes.

3. **Quadads**; these are chords containing four particular notes.

On account of groups of three (which are the mostly used harmony types in rock, pop, and different classifications) and quads, it is usually the situation we work the chords of stacked thirds (as recently talked about). On account of dyads, however, we can use any interval. Any Chromatic interval is additionally a dyad harmony, so they can be any major, minor, great, enlarged, or decreased dyads. The most widely recognized dyads in rock are dyads delivered by playing two notes, a fifth separated. Root and the immaculate fifth (now and again followed by another Root an Octave, on top). We call this "**Power chords,**" and are usually used by guitarists in rock and metal types.

It is conceivable to play a harmony comprising just 2 notes (and even of only 2 tones) and likewise of multiple notes. It isn't phenomenal for a jazz musician to play chords comprising 5 or 6 different notes, and piano players can perform upwards of 10 particular notes, one after another. We maintain this as a strategic distance, because the more one add the specific notes to harmony, the more they will conflict with one another, and the harmony will sound increasingly noisy. Most pop tunes have a straightforward harmony comprising basic chords with few notes, while jazz on the other range is exceptionally propelled harmony with progressively complex chords.

Understanding Chord Qualities And especially when discussing groups of three and quadads, chords have different flavors that portray them. These flavors are generally called **chord potentials**, and they make the chords sound different, not in the details of the sequential pitch, yet as far as the mood or the impact they produce. For instance, the most widely recognized harmony characteristics are major and minor, and the difference between them is anything but difficult to see: major chords are glad sounding, while minor chords are tragic sounding. **E** Major sounds very different from **E** minor, not similar as **E** Major would sound different from **F** Major, where harmony quality is the equivalent; however, the pitch of the root note is modified by one semitone.

The 'quality' that harmony will have altogether relies upon the interval structure (spelling) of that harmony, and each harmony, as we stated, has a one of a kind arrangement of intervals and a formula that portrays how it identifies with its scale. In the following few areas, we'll go over each harmony quality for sets of three and quadads. Note that when we state 'harmony quality,' we regularly avoid 'quality' and mostly allude to it as a 'harmony' — this fair implies we have relegated none of the 12 notes to the harmony yet. Before the finish of this chapter, you will have an enormous library of chords available to you and more than strong harmony establishment; and it will be anything but difficult to recall them all with the stunts I'll show you.

Set of three Chords

We'll begin with 3-note chords first because they are the least complex and most effortless to understand. They're the most well-known chords today. It merits repeating the most part when we talk about sets of three; we are discussing those ternions made of two 3rds (either major third or minor third interval) stacked on top of each other, or that are straightforward modifications of those stacked-third sets of three.

Set of three chords are as per Major triad

These chords comprise a: Root, a Major third, and a Perfect fifth. This implies we make them out of a root, a major third over that root, and a minor third over that subsequent note. Notice here that the proper ways from a Major third to a Perfect fifth is 3 semitones which is a minor third interval. The harmony formula for a major ternion is 1 3 5. In **C**, the **C** major ternion would be: **C E G.**

Minor Ternions

We make these of a minor third interval and a third major interval stacked besides (the backward of the organization of major groups of three). That implies that they comprise a Root, a minor third and a Perfect fifth. Concerning the minor set of three harmony formula first, we have a root 1, at that point, we have a minor third at that point; we have a minor third rather than a major third. These two intervals are one semitone separated, so that implies to get the minor third we need to flatten the third major note by a semitone, so we write b3. And then we have an ideal fifth. Likewise, note that the separation between the minor third and a perfect fifth is 4 semitones, which is a third major interval. So, a minor set of three harmony formulas is essential: **1 b3 5.** From our **C** major harmony comprising notes: **C E G,** we would get C minor with the notes: **C Eb G.** You can see here how just one note difference as meager as one semitone separated changes the mood of the harmony drastically. It goes from cheerful sounding (major) to miserable sounding (minor). We can presume that third in harmony is a significant note that has a huge effect on its sound. Regarding sets of three, there are too.

Expanded groups of three

These are major ternions with a sharp fifth. That implies they are worked from two major thirds stacked over each other and contain the notes: Root, Major third, **augmented fifth** (same as a minor sixth). Their sound is shaking (something to be thankful for), and these are once in a while played. The expanded set of three harmony formula is **1 3 #5. #5** advises that we need to raise the ideal fifth note by one semitone. Concerning the notes, **C Augmented**, or just Caugé would be: C E G#.

Decreased sets of three

These are minor sets of three with a flat fifth (Tritone). We make them out of two minor thirds stacked on each other, which implies they comprise a Root, a minor third, and a lessened fifth. The lessened harmony formula is **1 b3 b5,** which advises that we need to flatten both the third and fifth note of the parent scale. The C lessened harmony, or just Cdim, would then be **C Eb Gb.** We make these four essential groups of three out of two intervals, major and minor 3rds stacked over each other in different stages.

Suspended Chords

It is normal, however, to adjust those sets of three marginally and land at chords that are gotten from stacked 3rds yet that contain different intervals. This is finished by modifying the second note in those sets of three to the third, regardless of whether it is a major third or a minor third. We call these new chords Suspensions, and there are two kinds of them. There are suspended chords in which it brings down the third to a second. We call these Suspended second chords, or just sus2.

Suspended second Ternions

If you start with a major or minor set of three and lower the third to a major second, at that point, you will have a sus2 group of three. It comprises a Root, a Major second and a Perfect fifth, and we work it from an ideal fourth stacked over a major second interval.

The harmony formula for a sus2 harmony is **1 2 5**. This implies the notes of Csus2 harmony would be: **C D G** (we take the second note rather than the third from the C major scale).

Suspended fourth sets of three

The other suspended set of three is one in which we will raise the third to a fourth (instead of bringing down to a second). We call these the Suspended fourth chords and we ordinarily use it in jazz just as in rock and fly to include specific shading to major and minor set of three movements, that is neither major nor minor. Starting with a major or minor set of three, Sus4's are inferred by raising the second note in harmony (major or minor third) up to an ideal fourth. We work it from a major second interval stacked over an excellent fourth (something contrary to sus2), and we make it out of a Root, a Perfect fourth, and a Perfect fifth. The harmony formula for a sus4 harmony is **1 4 5**. The notes of Csus4 harmony would be **C F G**.

This finishes up many groups of three chords. It is likewise conceivable to discuss suspensions of decreased and increased chords — even though these are once in a while used. In these cases, the suspended chords have the same characteristics from previously; just the fifth is flatted (on account of a suspension of a decreased harmony) or sharped (on account of a suspension of an increased harmony). These chords appeared in the accompanying manner:

- dimsus4 (1 4 b5),

- dimsus2 (1 2 b5),

- augsus4 (1 4 #5),

- augsus2 (1 2 #5).

Out of these chords, the dimsus4 is very conflicting because there is just a half-advance difference between the Perfect fourth and reduced fifth. Investigate this table for an unmistakable diagram of the considerable number of chords;

Chords	Formulas			Notes in C
Major	1	3	5	C E G
Minor	1	b3	5	C Eb G
Augmented	1	3	#5	C E G#
Diminished	1	b3	b5	C Eb Gb
Suspended 2nd	1	2	5	C D G
Suspended 4th	1	4	5	C F G
Augsus 2	1	2	#5	C D G#
Dimsus 2	1	2	b5	C D Gb
Augsus 4	1	4	#5	C F G#
Dimsus 4	1	4	b5	C F Gb

Table 10: Trial chord

Chords	Notes											
	R	m2	M2	m3	M3	P4	dim5	P5	Aug5	M6	m7	M7
Major	R				M3			P5				
Minor	R			m3				P5				
Augmented	R				M3				Aug5			
Diminished	R			m3			dim5					
Suspended 2nd	R		M2					P5				
Suspended 4th	R					P4		P5				
Augsus 2	R		M2						Aug5			
Dimsus 2	R		M2				dim5					
Augsus 4	R					P4			Aug5			
Dimsus 4	R					P4	dim5					

Table 11: Triad chords interval structure

Set of three chords interval structure

This finishes up all harmony ternions. They are the most fundamental chords of the harmony worked in third—called: **Tertian harmony**—which a large majority of chords we hear today depend on. They are easy to learn and to be remembered. Likewise, there are first and second reversals for every one of these sets of three chords. However, we can't seem to go over the reversals.

7th Chords (Quadads)

More confounded than sets of three, because of additional note, 4-note chords, or quads, can be clarified just as broadened groups of three by another third — mostly, the **7th** or some likeness thereof. That is the reason they're regularly called seventh chords. Seventh chords contain 4 unmistakable notes; consequently why they're considered as quads.

We can work Quadads in more different manners than groups of three (since there is an additional note, which implies there are progressively potential mixes). However, they are mostly different variants of the

215

seventh chords (which comprise a Root, a third, a fifth, and a seventh). Quad harmony has more things going on, more notes conflicting with each other; it is hence progressively unpredictable and modern. We use broadly quadads over all others, yet particularly in blues and jazz. Seventh chords are as per:

▸ **Major 7**—these chords have a third major interval, trailed by a minor third, which is hunted by another major third on top. This implies they have a Root, Major third, Perfect fifth, and a Major seventh. Harmony formula is **1 3 5 7**. In C, the notes of **C Major7** harmony, or just **CMaj7**, or even **CM7**, would be: **C E G B**.

▸ **Minor 7**—we make these chords out of a minor third, trailed by a major third, followed by another minor third. So, they have the accompanying notes: Root, minor third, Perfect fifth, and a minor seventh. Harmony formula is **1 b3 5 b7**. In C, C minor 7, or Cm7, would be **C Eb G Bb.**

▸ **Dominant 7**—these chords resemble in the center between the past two. They have a Root, Major third, Perfect fifth, and a minor seventh. So, the major third is followed by two minor third intervals. Although they are the same as Major and minor seventh chords, they sound different, frequently adding pressure, which will cause general determination in a harmony movement. Harmony formula is **1 3 5 b7**. **C** prevailing 7, or only **C7** (as it's typically composed), has the notes: **C E G Bb.**

216

- **Minor 7b5**—this name may appear to be terrifying, yet it's in reality only a minor seventh harmony with a flat fifth. It's made from a: Root, minor third, reduced fifth (Tritone), and a minor seventh. This implies they have a minor third interval followed by another minor third, trailed by a major third (something contrary to Dominant 7). These are one of a kind sounding chords, regularly used in jazz, once in a while in blues, not as much in pop, rock, and similar styles. Harmony formula is **1 b3 b5 b7.** C minor 7b5, or Cm7b5, has the notes: C Eb Gb Bb.

- **Diminishes 7**—additionally **called Full Diminished**, these chords go above and beyond.

We make them distinct from stacked **minor** third intervals, which is the reason they are called **symmetrical chords.** Their interval structure is consistently the equivalent, no matter if you're ascending or descending in pitch. Practically, this implies you can move these chords up or somewhere around a minor third interval (3 semitones) as much as you need, and the notes would continue as before, just in different requests. Each note along these lines can go about as a root note. We regularly uses this in playing to get a cool sounding grouping, and jazz players specifically prefer to abuse this, though. Any chords that have similar intervals over the entirety of their notes are even. Enlarged ternions, for example, made up of two stacked major third intervals, are additionally even chords.

The sound of lessened 7 chords is bumping, dim and shaky, yet additionally intriguing and regularly used (cautiously) for emotional impact. Lessened 7 chords do not have to mix up with lessened ternions, which are called 'lessened.' They comprise a Root, minor third, reduced fifth, and major sixth. Harmony formula **is 1 b3 b5 bb7.**

NOTE: bb7 is a twofold flatted seventh, which implies that it is equivalent to the sixth scale degree by and by. C reduced 7, or Cdim7 for short, has the notes: C Eb Gb A.

- ▶ **Major 6**; these chords have a cool, unmistakable sound and we use it regularly in jazz, and once in a while in some different styles. We can use it to flavor up a standard major group of three, or as a substitute for a Major seventh, which can once in a while conflict with the melody if it's playing the root note— because the seventh note in a Major seventh harmony is just a semitone separated from the root. Their utilization is particular, and it is essential to investigate and trust your ears when it sounds great to use them. They comprise a major third, trailed by a minor third, and then a major second interval (which is 2 semitones). They have the notes: Root, Major third, perfect fifth, Major sixth. Harmony formula is **1 3 5 6. C Major 6,** or just **C6,** would **be C E.g. A.**

- ▶ **Minor 6**—at long last, sixth minor quads are a similar Major sixth, aside from with a minor third. They have a minor third interval followed by a major third, which is at that point, followed by a major second interval. They contain the notes: Root, minor third, Perfect fifth, Major sixth. Harmony formula is **1 b3 5 6. C minor 6,** or Cm6, would **be C Eb G A.** This finishes

218

up the principle quadad chords. These are not all conceivable blends of intervals that quads can comprise; there are many more you can make, for example, Dominant 7 harmony with a flat fifth (1 3 b5 b7). These might sound great in different circumstances, so consistently use your ear as a direction and recollect the brilliant principle: "If it sounds great, it is good."

Three Fundamental Chord Qualities

As we've seen, there are a lot of different harmony characteristics, yet there is a simple approach to arrange them all as per their sound and capacity in a harmony movement. This, additionally, goes for expanded and adjusted chords we will look at after this segment. There are three major harmony characteristics that all other harmony characteristics fall into. These are:

1. Major chords

2. Minor chords

3. Dominant chords

Here are few standards and rules to know which family harmony has a place with: If a harmony has a Major third and a Major 7th, then it is undoubtedly in the Major family. These chords are commonly cheerful sounding, and they can give security in a major key and provide a setting for melodic guidance in a harmonious movement. If harmony has a minor third note in it, at that point, we view it as a piece of the minor family. These chords are commonly dark sounding, something contrary to Major, and their work is likewise to give security, however, in a minor key. If a harmony has a Major third alongside a minor

219

seventh, at that point, it is unquestionably in the dominant family. We typically use dominant chords as quadads — they are major sets of three with the expansion of a minor seventh. We use these chords in all blues and many types — they make a great deal of pressure, to be settled in a harmony movement.

From these three fundamental chords, we can achieve every single other harmony. By changing notes of those chords or adding notes to them (as a rule as "augmentations" — thirds stacked over the chords), and then by subtracting different notes away from the subsequent chords, it is conceivable to create every other applicable harmony. For every one of these reasons, many musicians, even in jazz, consider each harmony an individual from either the major, minor or dominant family.

The Intricacy of Extensive chords (7s 9's, 11's and 13's)

Chords develop and advance past an octave, and when they do as such – when they contain a note which is a third up from the seventh (and hence higher than the octave) – they are usually called expanded chords. These chords are viewed as straightforward expansions of sets of three and quadads (with quadads being the augmentations of groups of three); and since these are commonly worked in thirds, the essential augmentations of the:

- **7th chords** (1 3 5 7) are different varieties

- **9th chords** or 9's (7's with a stacked third),

- **11th chords** or 11's (9's with another stacked third),

- **13th chords** or 13's (11's with another stacked third).

When broadening chords, we first take a look at the scale and expand its notes past the octave.

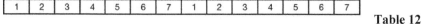

Table 12

The octave is the eight-note on a 7-note scale. So when a scale begins again at 1, we can write the number 8 instead of showing this is the octave with which the scale begins again — just an octave higher. At that point, we keep composing the numbers all together from that point. This implies the ninth note will be equivalent to the second; the tenth will be equal to the 3rd, 11th, same as 4th, 13th same as 6th, and so forth.

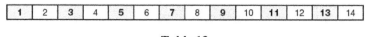

Table 13

If we have our typical 1 3 5 7 harmonies and expand it by a third, we would land on the ninth; if we expand that by another third, we would get to the eleventh, and if we broaden that by a third we would get to the thirteenth. So, the request wherein the chords expand is: Sets of three (**1 3 5**) - > **7th chords** (regularly as quadads) **1 3 5 7** - > **9's (1 3 5 7 9)** - > **11's (1 3 5 7 9 11)** - > **13's (1 3 5 7 9 11 13).**

In Summary: Adding 3rds to third based sets of three gives us seventh chords. Because these chords (ordinarily) contain four notes, they're quadads. With ternions, seventh chords structure the establishment of the third based (Tertian) harmony. We do not consider 7th chords "broadened chords," but we see them as ternion expansions.

For harmony to be an all-encompassing harmony, it needs to contain the notes that past the octave. Adding 3rds to 7's gives us 9's. These can be 5-note chords; however, some extra notes of a harmony that don't influence the sound much are precluded. This goes for 11's and 13's.

Adding 3rds to 9's gives us 11's.

And adding 3rds to 11's gives us 13's, in which the entirely broadened chords are, because they contain 7 particular notes in them. It's critical to realize that we do not play or voice all chords with these notes being incorporated — with the goal that it is conceivable to play the 7th harmony for case (which comprises a root, a third, a fifth and a seventh) by playing just a root, a third and a seventh, and forget about the fifth. It is exceptionally regular for notes to be let well enough alone for the harmony this way, and there are different explanations behind such. Sometime, it is physically challenging to play every of the note in harmony. Yet, sometime, forgetting about the notes that are not vital will make the harmony sound clearer and increasingly articulated. Having an excessive number of notes in harmony makes it sound swarmed, hazy, and confounding. So, evacuating these additional notes and lessening the harmony to a quadad (or even a set of three) is ideal because it makes the harmony sound increasingly engaged, more transparent, and better because fewer notes are conflicting with each other. There are sure "rules" about which notes can be let alone for harmony and which can't; we'll deal with them in a piece.

222

Note that we stop at the thirteenth note because if we were to add another third to our broadened harmony, we would land on the fifteenth note, and this note is equivalent to the first note of the harmony, just two octaves higher. This means stacking thirds after the thirteenth would only get us similar notes we had in our 1 3 5 7 harmonies. Since this wouldn't give us any new notes, there is no reason for broadening any further.

Another significant thing to know is that the centerpiece of the harmony is up to the seventh note. There are varieties of these chords, as we've seen, and every piece has a name. Any further expansions beyond the seventh are handled and treated differently. We do this in a manner so that there are just three fundamental varieties of each all-encompassing harmony: Major, minor, and Dominant. The all-encompassing chords are as per:

▶ **Major 9**—these are so cool, marvelous sounding chords. They comprise a Root, Major third, perfect fifth, major seventh, Major ninth (same note as the Major second just an octave higher). We make them out of intervals like a Major 7 harmony (major third—minor third—major third), with another minor third included at the top. Harmony formula is **1 3 5 7 9**. **C Major 9, or CMaj9,** would have the notes: **C E G B D**; although the fifth note (G for this situation) is regularly let alone for this harmony (just as all other expanded chords).

▶ **Minor 9**—correspondingly to Minor 7 chords, these offer similar intervals; we just need to include another major third too.

They comprise a Root, minor third, Perfect fifth, minor seventh, major ninth. Harmony formula is 1 b3 5 b7 9. C minor 9, or just Cm9, would be C, Eb, G, Bb, D.

- 9; we use these chords regularly in a funk (dominant 9 is here and there alluded to as the 'funk harmony'), and obviously, jazz. Here, once more, we're including an interval the major third for this situation—over a dominant 7 harmony (to get to the ninth from the minor seventh). These chords comprise a Root, Major third, perfect fifth, minor seventh, and a Major ninth. Harmony formula is **1 3 5 b7 9**. C dominant **9**, or just **C9**, would be **C E G Bb D.** By and by, all 9's are a portion of my preferred chords to play on guitar.

▶ **Major 11;** these chords comprise a Root, Major third, Perfect fifth, Major seventh, Major ninth and Perfect eleventh (same as the Perfect fourth). Harmony formula is **1 3 5 7 9 11.** CMaj11 would be **Minor 11;** these contain a Root, minor third, Perfect fifth, minor seventh, major ninth, Impeccable eleventh. Harmony formula is **1 b3 5 b7 9 11. Cm11** would be **C Eb G Bb DF**.

▶ **Dominant 11;** these contain a Root, Major third, Perfect fifth, minor seventh, Major ninth, Immaculate eleventh. Harmony formula is **1 3 5 b7 9 11. C11** would be **C E G Bb DF.** Because 11's are 6-note chords, they can be extraordinarily illogical and challenging to play; we can diminish them to 4-note chords just by forgetting about the fifth and the ninth, which are (by principle) non-essential notes for these chords.

- **Major 13;** these contain a Root, Major third, Perfect fifth, Major seventh, Major ninth, Immaculate eleventh, Major thirteenth (same as Major sixth). That was a lot of notes. Harmony formula is **1 3 5 7 9 11 13.** CMaj13 has the notes: **C E G B D F A.**

- **Minor 13;** contain a Root, minor third, Perfect fifth, minor seventh, Major ninth, Perfect eleventh, Major thirteenth. Harmony formula is **1 b3 5 b7 9 11 13.** Cm13 has the notes: **C Eb G Bb D F A.**

- **Dominant 13;** finally, these chords contain a Root, Major third, Perfect fifth, minor seventh, Major ninth, Perfect eleventh, Major thirteenth. Harmony formula is **1 3 5 b7 9 11 13.** C13 has the notes: **C E G Bb D F A.** 13's are frequently difficult chords to use and play. It looks as if you're playing a full scale as a harmony. They happen with less frequency (with at least one notes excluded), yet when they do, they can zest for any movement here and there with a frightening impact.

Dominant Chord Alterations

Dominant chords are one of a kind in a manner because we usually do the chromatic modifications on these kinds of chords. This is because we plan these chords for pressure, which they include when they happen in a harmonious movement. The reason for adding changed notes to a dominant harmony is to give considerably progressively strain, which at that point needs to determine gravely to a steady harmony. Hence, it is evident that you will frequently observe adjusted notes on a dominant harmony.

▸ **b9 and #9;** Dominant 7 harmony comprises the notes: **R M3 P5 m7. b9** note is equivalent to a minor second. The name of this harmony is 7b9. C7b9 would **be C E G Bb Db.** On the opposite side, **#9** over the dominant 7 is uncommon because it is one of the most well-known adjusted chords used in a funk, blues, rock, and jazz. We elude it to as the **Hendrix harmony** (E7#9 explicitly because of the open E string on guitar). **#9** is equivalent to a minor third and having this note alongside a Major third and minor seventh creates an extremely out-of-control sounding harmony. In C, the notes of this harmony are C E G Bb Eb.

▸ **b11 and #11; b11**, as we are probably aware, it is equivalent to a Major third. This note is, as of now, a piece of the dominant seventh harmony.

▸ **#11** is equivalent to an augmented fourth note. The name of this changed harmony would be **9#11.** In C, this harmony would have the notes: C E G Bb D F#.

▸ **b13 and #13;** At long last, b13 in harmony gives us the minor sixth note. The name of this dominant harmony would be 11b13. The notes in C will be C E G Bb D F Ab. Raising the thirteenth by a semitone gives us the minor seventh, presently in the dominant harmony.

Borrowed Chords versus Altered Chords; Traditional versus Jazz View;

Remember when we said that altered chords could be challenge on harmony. The reason is that there are two different ways of taking a gander at them: traditional and jazz.

Before this chapter, we referenced that each scale delivers a lot of chords, all worked in thirds on every one of its notes and composed around the root note of that scale, which is the key that those chords have a place with. We still can't seem to go over this in detail in the following segments; however, this is essential to recollect now because in the old style perspective on changed chords, and harmony that has been changed with the goal that it contains at least one notes that are never again part of the unique scale, implying that the harmony never again fits the key, is viewed as an adjusted harmony.

Harmonies like this that sounds astounding and 'out of key' to an audience in a musical piece is likewise called an obtained harmony or non-diatonic harmony. This is just a harmony that is obtained from a parallel mode, subsequently the name. Parallel modes, if you recall, share a similar key (same tonal focus); however, have different parent scale. This procedure of obtaining chords from a **parallel mode** is called **modular trade** or modular blend. For instance, we have a harmony movement that is in the key of C major: **Cmaj7—Am7— Fmaj7—G7.**

If we change the F major harmony in the movement to an F minor, with the goal that it is: **Cmaj7—Am7—Fm7—G** We would be in the key of C major mostly, yet with one harmony that has a place to C minor key rather, and that would be Fm7 harmony. C Major and C minor are parallel modes, and we have obtained a harmony from a parallel aeolian mode (common minor scale) for this situation C minor. This obtained harmony in the old style seems likewise viewed as a changed harmony because the third major note of the F harmony (F A-C), has been brought by a semitone down to Ab in this manner making a modified F major harmony regarding the first key.

In the more present-day—jazz see, changed chords areas we have portrayed them so far. Here, the changed chords have different modifications that, more often than not, don't have a place with the first key, however now and then they do. For instance, in our past movement, we can change the Fmaj7 with the goal that it is: **Cmaj7—Am7—Fmaj7#11—G7** This **FMaj7#11** harmony comprises the notes: F A C E B, which are all found in the key of C major. In the old style, see this would not be considered as a changing harmony, while in the advanced jazz, see this is unquestionably a modified harmony. Remember this qualification whenever you use changed chords.

Changed Harmony—How Altered Chords are Used and where do they come from

Recall our weird companion on the **Altered scale**? This scale, if you don't recollect, is the seventh method of the melodic minor scale. The changed scale is helpful for some reasons, and jazz players specifically prefer to use it to play progressively refined chords and lead lines over those chords. We regularly make chromatic adjustments on a dominant harmony that takes steps to the steadiest harmony in a harmonious movement. This harmony regarding harmony works in movements (which we still can't seem to go over) is called working **dominant harmony.** Because the motivation behind this harmony is to include strain, we regularly include much increasing strain and dramatization by modifying it with modified notes. Settling this modified dominant harmony to the following harmony, which is steady, delivers a very charming, 'getting back home' kind of sound.

You can likewise play lead lines over this changed dominant harmony and use adjusted scale specifically over that harmony before it settles. This will bring about some very modern lead lines that never sound standard—lines which jazz players regularly use in their performances. So how about we perceive how to fabricate the applicable changed scale from a dominant harmony, how about we state C7.

C7 harmony has the notes:

C	E	Bb
R	3	b7

Table 14: C7 harmony has the notes:

We will include the entire changed notes workable for a dominant7 harmony: **b9, #9, b5** (same as #11), **#5** (same as b13). Note that we bar the fifth (G for this situation) because that is one of the note, we will change with **b5 and#5.** We have:

C	Db	D#	E	Gb	G#	Bb
R	b9	#9	3	b5	#5	b7

Table 14

The scale we got by including the changed notes looks untidy. We will clean it up, using enharmonic counterparts with the goal that we can mastermind all notes in sequential order requests.

C	Db	Eb	Fb	Gb	Ab	Bb
R	b9	#9	3	b5	#5	b7

Table 15

What we have made is the C-changed scale. Since this scale is the 7th method of the melodic minor scale, we realize that it is just a semitone beneath the parent melodic minor scale of this mode. This implies the parent melodic minor scale of an adjusted scale is found on its second degree. In the key C, and that would be Db. So, the parent melodic minor scale of C-changed is Db melodic minor, and C-changed is the seventh method of Db melodic minor. Parent melodic minor scale is straightforward to make sense of for this situation—you have to look one semitone over the root of a dominant 7 harmony to discover it. For model, parent melodic minor scale of G-adjusted scale (worked out of G7 harmony) is abdominal muscle melodic minor. For what reason would you need to do this? This is very helpful because it's usually simpler to think and imagine the scale in the setting of a melodic minor as opposed to a changed scale.

Note this is just done on dominant chords because they have the specific capacity in a movement, which is to develop strain directly when it gets settled. Have you seen the notes unaltered by the changes we had previously? It's the M3 (E) and b7 (Bb). If we had all the notes unaltered, we would get: Do you recollect which scale this is?

C	D	E	F	G	A	Bb
1	2	3	4	5	6	b7

Table 16

It's the Mixolydian mode. It is moreover once in a while referred to as the **Dominant scale** because it contains the Root, M3rd, and m7, which are all an unquestionable requirement to have in a dominant harmony. What adjusted scale does is that it changes all little notes in a dominant scale, except for 1, 3, and b7. That is the reason the changed scale works best, and we use it regularly over dominant chords. Major and minor sort of changed chords have their uses, yet these are a lot rarer. We use them mostly to create increasingly extraordinary, different shading sounds that flavor up a movement in an attractive manner as 'obtained chords' if they are out of key.

Changed Chords Built-in 4ths

We must work, but not all groups of three, from stacked 3rds. We've just observed that in the instance of suspensions, there are different intervals: 2nds and 4ths that are stacked on top of each other.

It is conceivable even to construct triads starting from the earliest stage, basing them totally on a non-third interval. Usually, we finish this with 4ths. In these cases, we work those chords are by stacking 4ths: Perfect 4ths, flat 4ths, and sharp 4ths, in different approaches to make triads or quadads.

The subsequent chords; typically used in jazz and present-day old-style music — comprise, when all is said and done, of roots, 4ths, 7ths, and

231

10ths (1 4 7 10), and they have very particular sounds and serve very unmistakable capacities. C quadad worked in 4ths would be:

C	D	E	F	G	A	B	C	D	E	F	G	A	B	C
1	2	3	4	5	6	7	8	9	10	11	12	13	14	15

Table 17

We can use these chords instead of or notwithstanding third based chords to accomplish an assortment of impacts, however, that typically implies moving into the domain of some much propelled harmony. How about we shift gears for a tad and clarify in more detail chords relationship to scale?

How Chords Come from Scales

Chords originate from scales; we produce them by scales and are scholarly, composed of notes from their originating scale. This means that a scale will infer a specific rundown of chords, those chords all being in the same key as that scale.

Chords that originate from a major (diatonic) scale are called **diatonic chords**. Each major scale key (recall — 12 notes so 12 keys) has it is very own arrangement of seven chords — those chords start and are based on a different scale note.

Making sense of the considerable number of chords in a major key is straightforward. Suppose that we need to make sense of the significant number of chords in the key of C major. First, we number a C major scale and go a tad past an octave (up to the thirteenth):

1	2	3	4	5	6	7	8	9	10	11	12	13
C	D	E	F	G	A	B	C	D	E	F	G	A

Tab 18

Chords, as we are probably aware, are regularly worked in thirds. Therefore, we will start by stacking thirds similarly as in the past. We will begin by including the third and the fifth note on each scale degree. This will bring about getting 7 different arrangements of 3 notes, and then we need to break down what harmony make up those notes; for instance, the first note in C major scale is C. At the point when you include the third and the fifth note to it; you get the notes: C E G. Second note in C major is D, in the wake of including the third and the fifth (considering from D the first note), you get: DF An, and so on.

Ways of Analyzing Diatonic Chords

1. **The primary gathering of notes we have is: C, E, G;**

   When we have a gathering of notes this way, and we need to make sense of what harmony it is, we start by contrasting the notes with the major scale of the base most minimal note. For this situation (C E G), it's C, so we investigate the C major scale. We see that these notes are completely found in the C major scale — they're the first, third, and fifth. We realize that harmony, which has 1 3 5 harmony formula, is major, so this must be C Major Harmony (making sense of this harmony is self-evident).

2. **Next gathering of notes is: D, F, A;**

Once more, we start by checking and contrasting the notes with the major scale of the base note. For this situation, it's D, so we check the D major scale.

D (1)	E (2)	F# (3)	G (4)	A (5)	B (6)	C# (7)	D (8)

Tab 19

We can see that D is the Root note, and An is the fifth note; however, F—the third note in our harmony—isn't found on a D major scale.

Rather, we have F#. This discloses to us that our note (F) flats by a semitone (a half-advance down on the note circle). At the point when we stack thirds (1 3 5) in a D major scale, we get the notes of a D major harmony: D F# A; however, since our third note is F, it implies that our harmony formula arrangement is really: 1 b3 5. And what sort of harmony has a formula: 1 b3 5; Minor harmony. So this must be D minor at that point.

3. **Next gathering of notes is: E, G, B;**

We check the E major scale and rehash the same procedure. In E major, the 1 3 5 notes are: E G# B. Since our third is G, it implies that, once more, this note got flatted by a semitone, and the formula grouping for E G B is: 1 b3 5. This tells us that the third harmony is another minor harmony, and its E minor (in the key of C major). I'll let you make reason the harmony for the following three-note gatherings: F A C; G B D; A C E; You need to follow a similar procedure as depicted for the initial two-note gatherings.

If you experience any difficulty somewhat further in this segment, there will be a complete rundown with all C major scale chords so you can check to ensure you took care of a business. I needed to clarify the last gathering of 3 notes beginning the seventh level of the C major scale — **B DF.** When we check the major scale of the base note:

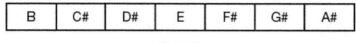

B	C#	D#	E	F#	G#	A#

Tab 20

We can see that both the third (D) and the fifth (F) in our note bunch are a semitone lower than the third and the fifth in the B major scale. This implies rather than 1 3 5; we have 1 b3 b5. Do you recollect what sort of harmony has this formula? You've gotten it — it's a decreased one!

Amassing Diatonic Chords

To condense what we have so far, here's a rundown of chords we have by breaking down the notes:

Scale degree	R	3	5	Chord
1	C	E	G	C major
2	D	F	A	D minor
3	E	G	B	E minor
4	F	A	C	F major
5	G	B	D	G major
6	A	C	E	A minor
7	B	D	F	B diminished

Tab 21

Diatonic Chords in C Major Scale

Each key of the major scale produces 3 Major chords, 3 minor chords, and has one lessened harmony, which begins the seventh scale degree! There is just a single difficulty with this, and it's that, in reality, the notes are not given continuously in this right set of three requests. Here and there, we use a harmony reversal (we talk about those next) where the root note isn't the most reduced note in harmony. For instance, you can have notes: **F A D**, and it may appear to be befuddling to figure out the harmony. It is a various thing; however, this is essentially the reversal of **D minor (D F A).**

Here's another model: **B G# E.** Would you be able to figure this harmony? It's E major, yet with the turnaround note request. Perceiving these chords by their notes when they're in a reversal, is something you will be better at as you gain experience playing and making sense of stuff with no one else. Great beginning is to become accustomed to the normal harmony note groups with the goal that when you see one with a different note request, you can, in a split second, recall its exact harmony.

The basic ones are:

CEG (C harmony), GBD (G), FAC (F), ACE (Am), EGB (Em), DF#A (D), AC#E (A), BD#F# (B), EG#B (E), BbDF (Bb), BDF# (Bm), DFA (Dm).

In a further developed harmony where increasingly complex chords (with more notes) are used, it will be more enthusiastically to do this because we can forget a few notes. This can make a great deal of

236

disarray concerning what sort of harmony it is, however, there are strategies to make sense of even those, it's only somewhat progressively confounded. Returning to our scale harmony, you need to recall that each major scale key will create this equivalent arrangement of harmony characteristics. Here is the major scale ternion harmony succession:

Maj	min	min	Maj	Maj	min	dim
I	ii	iii	IV	V	vi	vii

Tab 22

We should keep this succession. Each major key will deliver this equivalent succession of a set of three chords.

Note that scale degrees are generally written in roman numerals. This is significant because of the harmony movements we will discuss later. The diatonic quadads harmony grouping is comparable, however, with somewhat different harmony characteristics:

Maj7	min7	min7	Maj7	(Dom)7	min7	min7b5
I	ii	iii	IV	V	vi	vii

Tab 23

We realize that these seventh quadads are the chords you get including another third over a set of three chords. You can undoubtedly make sense of the diatonic quadads by yourself and think of the same chords from in this succession. In cases of unforeseen issue, if you need any help, how about we do it together for the V harmony (Dominant 7) and for the vii harmony (min7b5) because we haven't had them in diatonic triads.

Dominant 7 harmony is the harmonies we get if stack the thirds beginning from the fifth scale degree. On account of the C Major scale, the fifth degree is G, so we fabricate our dominant harmony over this note. We take the first, third, fifth, and a seventh (four notes because it is a quadad harmony), however beginning from the G note. We get the notes: G, B, D and F. At that point we check the G major scale and see that G is the Root.

Major 3rd, D is the Perfect 5th; however, the seventh note is F#, and we have F. This implies that a semitone flats the seventh note, and what we have is the harmony formula for a Dominant 7 harmony: **1 3 5 b7**. In quadad structure, min7b5 is the harmony we get when we stack the thirds beginning from the seventh major scale degree. If we do this in the key of C major, we get the notes: B, D, F, and A. At that point we check these notes in B major scale—B is the **Root, D#** the third (we have D), F# is the fifth (we have F), and A# is the seventh (we have A). So, all notes after the root have got flatted by a semitone. This implies that the harmony formula for this harmony is: 1 b3 b5 and b7. In ternion structure, this was a reduced harmony (or half-decreased to be exact); however, when we include another third on top, it becomes min7b5.

Note that our reduced seventh, or full decreased harmony, with the formula: 1 b3 b5 bb7, is certifiably not a diatonic harmony because it doesn't show up in this diatonic succession of 4-note chords. We can do this specific procedure to make sense of the chords that are found in a minor Scale, yet we don't need to. We realize that a minor scale is essentially the sixth method of a major scale, so we should take the major scale harmony grouping and reorient it, and we start from the vi harmony. By doing so, we get the minor scale set of three harmony arrangement:

min	dim	Maj	min	min	Maj	Maj
i	ii	III	iv	v	VI	VII

Tab 24

In the key of A minor (the sixth method of C major) that would be: **A min (i), B diminish (ii), C Maj (iii), D min (iv), E min (v), F Maj (vi), G Maj (vii).** You can apply this minor harmony succession to any common minor key, and you would get the chords in that key.

Transposing from One Key to Another

The need to play in a lot of different keys isn't extraordinary for a musician. Having the option to change keys on the spot is a constructive attitude to have for an assortment of reasons — particularly if you need to play chords on your instrument. Most times, the explanation behind the reason we do this is because we need to play in a key that better suits a vocalist's voice (doesn't make a difference if we sing or another person), or it may be progressively helpful to play in a specific key contingent upon a circumstance. Regardless, having this ability is very helpful and significant, mainly if you are playing in a band.

Fortunately, since you already know the arrangement of chords that each major scale produces, changing starting with one key then onto the

239

next is quick and straightforward. If we have a harmony grouping playing, for instance: **C — Am — F — G**, we make sense of that, and these are **I — VI — IV — V** chords of the C major key. If we need to change keys to G, first we have to make sense of the chords in the key of G, and then apply this harmony movement.

1. **G major scale is: G, A, B, C, D, E, F#**

2. In the wake of applying the formula: Maj, min, min, Maj, Maj, min, diminish, we get the accompanying chords: **G Maj (I), A min (ii), B min (iii), C Maj (IV), D Maj (V), E minor (vi), F# diminish (vii).**

3. At that point, we should apply I — **vi** — **IV** — **V** harmony arrangement to the key of G, and we get the chords: **G — Em — C — D.** So, what was **C — Am — F — G** in the key of C is now **G — Em — C — D** in the key of G. This should be possible in all keys and with any harmony movement.

Harmony Inversions and Chord Voicing

We regard the course of action of notes in harmony as a **harmony voicing**. Therefore, it speaks to the request and the frequency by which the notes show up in harmony when we play it. By frequency, I mean how often we rehash the notes in a harmony played. For instance, an E Major group of three comprises the notes: **E G# B**. This is a model of an essential harmony voicing. The notes are going from lower to higher all together, so that E—the Root, is the least note, G# is the Major third and higher in pitch E, and B—the Perfect fifth is the highest note in this voicing. However, now and then we can play a harmony wherein the request for the notes differs from this one, so that, for instance, we can have: E B G #and it may not be clear from the start that this is as yet an E major ternion, however, with a different voicing. E (Root) is as yet the most minimal note, yet now G# (Major third) is the most noteworthy note in this voicing.

This is regularly the situation on a guitar where harmony can have various shapes and ways it very well may be played, each with a different harmony voicing (and additionally different fingering decisions). If we retake our E major ternion and play it on guitar as a fundamental open harmony shape, we can see that the request for the notes played from most reduced to most elevated is: **E(R), B(P5), E(Octave), G# (M3), B(P5), E(Double Octave).** This is a case of a harmony voicing where E note seems to appear multiple times (in **3 octaves), B (P5)** shows up twice, and the **G# (M3)** shows up just once. We can see that one harmony can have a wide range of voicing, and Root is consistently the bass (most minimal) note. However, there are uncommon situations when it's not.

Most all chords are third-based. The general harmony type is with the end goal that it contains a root followed by a progression of stacked thirds (major or minor) that make the characteristics of that harmony. It is conceivable, however, to deliver chords that don't have this structure, however, are as yet dependent on thirds. This is finished by re-masterminding the notes of a stacked third harmony in a manner so that the most reduced note in harmony, the bass note is never again the root note (that implies that the root note is contained somewhere else in harmony). We designate these chords **"Reversals."** We can say that a harmony reversal is voicing a harmony note other than the Root as its most minimal note. The easiest reversals are ternion reversals (because those are the least difficult chords). For any group of three, since there are three unmistakable notes, there are two particular reversals that can be created (notwithstanding the first harmony, where the root note is the bass note).

Reversals of 7ths and Extended Chords

It is conceivable to rearrange 7ths and broadened chords in an assortment of approaches to wind up with harmonically complex chords. For any quadad, since there are 4 unmistakable notes, there are three unmistakable reversals (that follow a similar rationale as a set of three reversals) in which the Root isn't the most minimal note, and continue as more notes are included.

Ordinary Root position **(1 3 5 7)**—Root is the most reduced note first reversal **(3 5 7 1)**—third is the bass note, and Root is the most noteworthy note second reversal **(5 7 1 3)**—fifth is the bass note, and Root is the second most remarkable note third reversal **(7 1 3 5)**—seventh is the bass note. The root is the second most reduced note. These chords, frequently used in contemporary old-style music and jazz, are valuable for some reasons, most clearly as substitution chords. Remember that you can have any harmony voicing, which means any note request in harmony, yet as long as the Root is as the most minimal note, then it isn't thought about a reversal.

Ways of Finding Root Note Position in a Rearranged Chord

We frequently mastermind harmony voicing in a manner with the goal by taking a gander at the notes and it is a long way from clear what harmony it is. Fortunately, there is a simple strategy to discover where the root note is in a previously altered voicing that you may get. The technique is just to revise the notes until we stack them in third, in order, and this is because we work most of the chords in thirds. Suppose we have a harmony voicing with the accompanying notes (all together from most reduced to most elevated): **A, F#, A, D, F#,** and we need to make sense of where the Root is and what harmony this is.

1. **First, we perceive that there** are just three unmistakable notes in this harmony, so this must be a set of three or the like. We likewise dismiss any #'s or b's because we only need to make sense of the thirds one after another in order.

2. **At that point, we stack a third over each note**, beginning from the least, which for this situation is A. A third up from An, if we check one after another in order (**A, B, C—1, 2, 3**), is the C note. We check if this note coordinates the note alongside An in our harmony. It doesn't since the following note is F#.

3. **As we proceed onward to the following note—F#.** We dismiss the sharp, so a third up from (F, G, A—1, 2, 3) is A note. This is great because A matches the following note in our harmony. This implies F# could be the beginning note. At that point, we include a third up from A, which, once more, is the C note, and it doesn't coordinate the next note, which is D. Seems F# isn't the root note.

4. **At that point, we proceed onward to D.** A third up from D is F. It matches. We add a third to F and get A note. Match once

more. Since this is a ternion, it's enough to get two matches in push (for quadads, you would require three matches). We reclaim the sharps or flats to all notes that had them. For this situation, just F had a sharp. The notes we got by revamping them in thirds are D F# An, and these are the notes of a D Major harmony. A note was at the base as the most minimal note; it implies this is the second reversal of D Major Harmony. This procedure is straightforward, and you can use it whenever you're uncertain what harmony you're confronting. Regarding triads, you need to keep an eye out for those suspensions (second and fourth). If any of the notes with a stacked third doesn't coordinate, attempt to check up in order by a second and a fourth. For a sus2 harmony first, discover a note coordinate with the stacked second and then with a stacked fourth and then with stacked second note. As the quantity of the notes in harmony expands, it gets continuously more difficult to make sense of the harmony, besides harmony can sometimes have a few different names—the decision of which will rely upon the general harmony you were given (or not).

Slash Chords

Slash chords are the strategy we used to record transformed chords. They look as two-letter names isolated by a forward slash. Here, the note on the upper left speaks to the harmony, and the note on the base right speaks to the harmony note is in the bass as the most reduced note. For this situation, G is in the bass of the C Major7 harmony. This harmony has the notes: C (1), E(3), G(5), B(7), so what we have is the second reversal of the CMaj7 harmony. In a band circumstance, bass player ordinarily covers the most minimal note of slash chords; and then a harmony player can easily play a standard non-upset harmony. We do not merely use the slash chords for documenting altered chords. They are the vast majority of the time; however, they can have different uses as well.

One such example is the point at which we have a slash harmony wherein the base right note isn't a piece of the harmony on the upper left. For instance, G/F# is revealing to us we need to play a G major set of three over the F# note in the bass. We typically view this as terrible documentation practice because you don't acknowledge from the outset what harmony it is that you're playing in a harmony movement. This confines your choices as an entertainer and settles on it harder to use sound judgment regarding voice driving and how to move to start with one harmony then onto the next.

Voice Leading (music production)

With every chord we had so far, you may think about the reason for harmony reversals, and as it should be. There is one principal motivation behind why musicians use them, and it comes down to voice driving.

Voice driving is a more established term that originates from choral music. This is the music composed for ensembles—a musical gathering comprising just vocalists. In this music, each voice (vocalist) has a distinctive melody line, and the way this melody line moves and collaborates with different voices in an ensemble is called voice driving.

Exciting, this means different ideas in music. For instance, if rather than vocalists, we had four different instruments, each playing an exclusive melody line, those tunes—comprising individual notes—would lead to make and diagram chords. Voice driving would be the procedure by which those songs move in harmony. Voice driving additionally means playing chords on a single instrument. Here, it is about how we interface chords together in a steady progression to make smooth melodic lines for each note in harmony as it moves to the following harmony. Suppose we play two or three 4-note chords in a harmony movement. We can think of each note as a different melody line that moves as one harmony changes to another harmony. The purpose of voice driving is to make melodic lines for each of the harmony notes that are smooth, simple to play and great sounding, so that the harmony movement sounds better and even more engaging to our ears. All together to do this, we need to focus on what every one of the harmony notes is doing. In the good 'old days, authors saw that moving between the notes that are closer to one another sounds better. So, mostly, when creating or masterminding harmony, we need to maintain a strategic distance from clumsy intervals and hops difficult to play and don't sound as high.

From this comes the fundamental rule of voice driving, which expresses that as the harmony changes, each voice (harmony note, for instance) ought to move, preferably, only one entire advance up or down in pitch. A note can continue as before between two chords, or it can move by a half-advance or progress, yet only that. We view this as a decent voice driving practice. This would deliver smooth sounding harmony changes that are increasingly melodic, and simpler to play and tune in to. A decent similarity for this would be the rhyme of the verses in tune—the words that rhyme resembles the harmony notes that move close to an entire advance as the harmony changes.

Polychords

It is conceivable to join chords to deliver new chords. We typically call these polychords. Regularly, these chords are perplexing and difficult to play over, yet they are helpful to some improvisers and arrangers for an assortment of reasons. Polychords, as the name implies, speak to two chords played simultaneously, with one being played over the other. They are the same as slash chords but different in two significant ways. Rather than with a forward slash, polychords are documented as a division with one harmony on top and the other on the base. The harmony on the base is the lower some portion of the polychord. We play the top harmony over the bass harmony.

Modulation and How Is It been Used

Particular from tonal focuses are key focuses. At the point when a key is transformed, we state that the melody has tweaked. In these cases, as opposed to a temporary harmonic focus being built up and then went through (on the way as a rule to the key of the melody), the whole harmonic structure of the movement shifts up or somewhere near some interval.

There are no immovable guidelines in pop or rocks that oversee the way modulation happens; however, when all is said and done, it happens toward the start of a reiteration of a few movements. That whole reiteration happens in the balanced key. To smooth the change, it is sometimes simple to supplant the harmony right away, going before the modulation with a dominant harmony from the new (regulated) key. Modulations are regular in popular music, nation, and rock, especially toward the end of a melody, where an abstain might rehash a full advance over the first root. This is one, straightforward, type of modulation rehashing a movement precisely as it was, just sequential. Regularly, this happens up as opposed to down, and it happens into equal parts steps, entire advances, or major third (two-stage) intervals. The finish of the Titanic signature melody is a case of this modulation.

The Significance of having a Good Rhythm

Barely any things in music (and maybe in life) are as significant as rhythm. Like so much jazz, funk, and blues musicians know, it is conceivable to play anything and have it sound great if you have the depression, the swing, the vibe, the stream. Developing rhythm is more than just understanding the numbers, it is about placing hours in with your instrument, truly getting settled with it, culminating your system, setting up an inside clock, and so forth. A portion of this is about challenging to grow inactively alone, and so playing with different musicians (who have extraordinary rhythm abilities) as regularly as would be prudent, circling yourself (recording you're playing) and using your circles to rehearse over (this will help analyze rhythmic issues) and playing to a metronome (particularly when you are first adopting some method or example) are all very significant. Playing moderate and concentrating on timing as opposed to on speed is additionally a significant portion of growing great rhythm. If you're playing moderate, you'll be practicing your timing, and if you're playing fast(er), your spotlight will be more on your speed. The get is that incredible sounding pace, playing, and fantastic method as we created it through moderate and connected with reiteration (you must have the timing down first) and with progressive speed increments. For every one of these reasons, understanding rhythm is an enormous piece of music theory on how time is isolated in music, how a heartbeat capacitate, how a musician can make and resolve strain, or recount to a story rhythmically. Understanding and disguising these things might be the most significant piece of being an entertainer or writer and sounding great, and it should be the most compensating part of your playing.

Understanding Time, Beat, Bar and Tempo

In music theory, "**time**" alludes to the beat or the beat of the music and its time signature. The **beat** of the music is the most fundamental unit of time. It is the thing we tap our foot, gesture our heads, or applaud to. The time signature of a piece characterizes it. A "**bar**," additionally called a "measure," is another key unit that measures the time of a piece against which note/we comprehend beat divisions. In the end, a bar is one complete cycle of the beats, and it is continuously characterized with signature. Bars are a helpful method for keeping the music sorted out into little pieces.

The **tempo** is another critical component of music. It portrays the speed at which the beats occur the beat of the music. It is usually communicated in beats per moment or BPM. It discloses to us the number of beats in a single moment (for model 80 bpm implies 80 beats for every moment).

Thinking about the time and the tempo of a piece as of now discloses to you pretty much step-by-step instructions to play over it, it as of now makes the mood of the piece apparent. If you discover nothing progressively about a piece going in, it is conceivable to ad-lib incautious, complex, and incredible ways, using your ear to direct your harmonic and melodic sense.

Simultaneously, if you don't understand what the time of a piece, it is anything but difficult to lose all sense of ways in the fight (regardless of whether you are playing a created piece or extemporizing).

Understanding time is of fundamental significance

Time Divisions

In music theory, **time** is separated numerically, as indicated by straightforward proportions. This is valid for time signatures, as we will see, and it is valid for the way that notes or **beats** are separated as a rule. We state that any note, held for some measure of time, has a specific worth, and that worth is communicated numerically. So this note esteem is a space of time in music with a particular length. In music, there are notes with the accompanying qualities: Entire note (a note held for the length of a standard **bar** in like manner time – more on this soon)

- **Half note** (held for half up to an entire note)

- **Quarter note** (held for a fourth of an entire note, or half of the half note)

- **Eighth note** (an eighth of an entire note, or half of the quarter note)

- **Sixteenth note** (a sixteenth of an entire note, or half of the eighth note).

These are the most widely recognized note esteems. There are likewise notes that are longer than entire notes (however once in a while utilized):

- **Twofold whole** notes (held for the length of two bars in like manner time)

- **Longa** (a note held for the length of four bars in like manner time)

- **Maxima** (a note held for an all-out length of eight bars in like manner time) And some notes are shorter than 16ths. Those are:

- **32nd note** (note with the worth equivalent to the half of the sixteenth note)

- **64th note** (half of 32nd)

- **128th note** (half of 64th)

- **256th note** (half of 128th)

It isn't extremely regular to experience notes, for example, longa or maxima, or notes any shorter than 16ths or 32nds aside from sometimes in structures played at a more slow tempo, however, with rapid runs.

Anytime in a musical piece, it is conceivable to play heaps of notes (sixteenth's and 32nd's) that sound quick while as yet keeping time and holding the moderate tempo of the piece (60 bpm or less). It is likewise conceivable to play just two notes (entire and half notes, for instance), although the tempo of the tune is rapid (120+ bpm). In the two cases, the rhythm gives the general emotional feel for the speed of the tune.

Notwithstanding fundamental divisions, any of these notes can turn into a spotted note (note with an essential speck '.' alongside it), which demonstrates that the length of the note is 1.5 times the ordinary length. For instance: **Dotted** entire note is one whole note + one-half notes (or three half notes):

▶ **Dotted** half note is one-half note + one-quarter note (or three-quarter notes).

▶ **Dotted** quarter note is one-quarter note + one eight-note (or three eight notes).

▶ **Dotted** eighth note is one-eighth note + one-sixteenth note (or three 16ths).

▶ **Dotted** sixteenth note is one-sixteenth note + one 32nd note, and so forth.

There are likewise n-tuplets, for example, triplets and pentuplets (or quintuplets), in which some number of notes are fit equitably into a measure of time. Eighth-note triplets, for example, provide 3 notes where there are two eighth notes (we'll get to them in apiece).

Polyrhythms and Polymeters

It is conceivable to make uncontrollably confusing time signatures. Since an arranger or then again improviser can move between time signatures (using one for some number of bars and then transforming it to something different), it is conceivable to make difficult, refined rhythmic cross-sections (as in "math rock," some metal, and some jazz). It is likewise significant that we can stack different time signatures over one another. At the point when we accomplish this, either a polyrhythm or polymeter — a propelled ideal results. Polyrhythms are two bars of a similar length being played while, have different time signatures (for example, a bar of 3/4 and a bar of 7/4, which take up a similar measure of time).

Polymeters work by consolidating two different time signatures with the goal that the length of each heartbeat is the equivalent (bringing about bars of different lengths that can cycle against one another throughout the stage). We use these things in present-day metal and math rock, in current jazz, in contemporary old-style music, and in cutting-edge act of spontaneity.

Ways of Creating Movement in Music; Timbre/Tone

An author or entertainer can use note choice to assemble and discharge pressure to make development. They can likewise use, as we have seen, note span — by controlling time, they can accomplish all the ways of intricacies. There are different methods for traveling through musical space, different tomahawks, other devices, different vehicles. One of these is timbre or tone shading.

Timbre and tone allude not to the pitch of a sound, and not to its volume, however, to what the sound sounds like. They are the character or the sound, the shading, or the nature of a sound. Although they are regularly used, conversely, "timbre" and "tone" are sometimes used to allude to different highlights of sound shading. In these cases, we list the timbre of a sound to whatever instrument we create the sound with, a violin's A note, which differs from a saxophone's An, and the difference between those two sounds is the timbre. The tone, then again, is the specific tonal nature of the sound turning out of that instrument, influenced by the arrangement of the instrument, the method, the amplification and any impacts used. When all is said and done, the timbre or the tone of a sound (and here we envision that those two things are the equivalent) is one manner in which an author or entertainer can control the feeling of a bit of music. We construct Pressure and discharged it by method for timbre, the same amount as for pitch or span.

Consonance and Dissonance

It is one thing to realize how to make music sound great — sound decent, satisfying, and simple to tune in to. It is one thing to have the option to play consonant (music that sounds like goals, that inclines toward decreased strain), yet it is another to be ready to make development in a piece genuinely. Genuine development requires that, as a general rule, we make offensive sounds — that is, sounds that tend towards pressure, sounds that are difficult, astounding, and even brutal. Using harmonic and melodic thoughts that advance discord, playing on the rhythm of a tune, and using syncopation in unforeseen manners using timbre, tone and elements to make pressure. These are altogether methods for delivering development in music.

Putting Musical Structures Together

The initial move toward building hypothetical mastery in music is learning your direction around the ground floor — understanding the key components of music, the theoretical structures that we work within music theory, and how those structures work together in some essential manners. This, however, is sufficiently just to get you to understand what music is made of, and in no sense how music works. Understanding music is endlessly more than understands the discrete components that make it up. Music is a moving, living, beating body, and simply like our bodies, its systems are final to any arrangement of straightforward components. The end game more than understands it is mastery and that comes from having the option to control musical structures, giving them something to do, and making them work for you in the manner you might want. An essential presentation is required first, which pretty much contains two parts:

- An overview of the fundamental components of music theory, its essential structures (concealed to this point);

- An approach to take care of those structures together to increase a more prominent understanding of what's going on in the genuine, material demonstration of music-production.

That subsequent undertaking is the thing that this segment is tied in with: giving you access on a portion of the insider facts of musical systems; giving you how musical components and structures bode well together; and preparing you for the following stage, which is a more extensive point of view — a further developed discussion about how to control hypothetical structures in your playing and composing. The purpose of this segment isn't to get you the entire route there, just to make you move morally justified bearing.

With that in mind, we will examine, initial, an expansive qualification among improvising and composition (to consider how improvisers and authors use music theory), second, a general scientific classification of music theory (or if nothing else of harmony as it is seen hypothetically), and third, a lot of musical thoughts and structures that are essential in your adventure toward hypothetical mastery.

How Chords Function in a Key

Each key has seven fundamental chords (one for each note in the scale). Each of these chords has a capacity. Be that as it may, for every one of the seven, there are just three fundamental capacities, just three fundamental groups: tonic, dominant, and subdominant. Tonic chords are the steadiest and they set up a key. They are the ones that harmony movements move to discharge strain. They are the main, third, and 6th degrees of whatever scale is at hand. **Dominant** chords are the tensest, and they need unequivocally to take steps to a few tonic harmonies. Dominant chords are the most remote, harmonically, away from the tonic; however, that implies that they point back toward the tonic. So they can lead the movement back to the key focus. These are the fifth and seventh degrees of the scale, and any chords based on those degrees.

Subdominant chords are the chords that build up development away from the tonic and toward the dominant before the dominant chords need to determine back to the tonic chords. Tonic chords set up a key, though subdominant chords move away from that key. These chords are tense, however, not similarly that dominant chords are, and they will generally advance toward dominant chords (although they can likewise switch bearings and move back toward tonic chords). These are the second and fourth degrees of the scale.

We should take a model, utilizing the key of C

In C Major, and harmony worked from the C major, E minor, or A minor triad which are thought about tonic chords. These chords will set up the key focus. Any chords based on the D minor or F major triads will move away from C major as a tonic. These are the subdominant chords, and they are consistently on the second and fourth degrees of the scale. At long last, any chords based on the G major or B reduced triads are dominant chords. These are consistently on the fifth and seventh degrees of a scale. These chords will build up the most strain, yet they will likewise point directly back to tonic chords since they need to determine toward that path.

How Notes Function in a Chord

The notes of a chord work in unsurprising manners, much the same as the chords of a key. The essential structure of the chord at its easiest, the triad, is the steadiest piece of that harmony, with the 1 and 5 being the most consonant. This is the reason it is conceivable to play only power chords (otherwise called fifth) and sound great. The 3 is a steady note in a chord, yet not as steady as the 1 or 5. The 3 does, however, decide if the harmony is major or minor.

The main augmentation of a triad is a 7. This is the following most stable interval after the 3, and it fills in also to shading the harmony and decide its family major, minor, dominant. The last three expansions **9, 11, 13** don't know when all is said and done, build up the establishment of that harmony, nor do they decide if it is a major, minor, or dominant Harmony. They are likewise far less steady than the **1, 3, 5, or 7** notes (those four are designated "harmony tones" decisively because of their dependability). These augmentations do, however, shading the Harmony in different ways minor sixth sounds very different from a major sixth, for example.

Kinds of Harmony

Harmony is immediately the most essential and the most exceptional idea in music theory. It is the bed stone of our opinion of when we guess, and it very well may be made to be more intricate than the vast majority anticipates. At the point when we talk about Harmony, we are discussing how that notes hang together, regardless of whether they are consonant or discordant, and what sorts of structures they can be organized into. We are likewise discussing the entirety of that

258

temporally outside of time. For chord, it doesn't make a difference to what extent notes are held, only that they are on the whole hanging together in a structure. It very well may be said that Harmony can be either:

1. **Tonal**

2. **Modular**

3. **Polytonal**

4. **Atonal**

Here's an outline of each.

Tonal Harmony

The vast majority of the music in the West is what designated "Tonal" music is, and it is in the territory of tonal Harmony. Tonal music will be music that has a tonic, or a key focus — a note that goes about as the focal point of gravity for the piece or the piece of the piece you're discussing. And tonal Harmony is how we understand the Harmony of tonal music — it comprehends chords and scales relative to a few key focus or tonic. Tonal Harmony can be either: chordal, scalar or chromatic.

Chordal

Chordal music will be music whose essential harmonic vehicle is the Harmony. We investigate it by dissecting how the chords move and collaborate. The most fundamental unit in chordal music is the

Harmony, and for the most part, this implies that we are discussing triads and their relationships.

Scalar

Scalar music will be music whose essential harmonic vehicle is the scale. We understand this music by dissecting how that notes and chords are determined from the scales that contain them. The most fundamental unit of harmonic in scalar music is a scale as opposed to Harmony, the last being determined as an individual from the previous. This implies by and large, we are discussing some scale or mode (or arrangement of scales and modes) instead of some provision of triads.

Chromatic

Chromatic music is comparable on a fundamental level to scalar music, just the scale that is utilized is the 12-tone chromatic scale. This implies, in theory that the music is free to leave the space of tonality and move into atonal Harmony (see atonal segment underneath), however by and by, it is regularly attached to some focal point of gravity.

Modular versus Tonal Harmony

Tonal music, as we have stated, is music in which there is a note that goes about as the focal point of gravity. This case is chordal or scalar (or chromatic), however in those cases, there is one note that burdens the music at any one time. Modular music is different — it accepts a scale or mode as a spot to start and treats all of the notes in that scale as the purposes of gravity. It might be said; the whole scale is the "key" or "tonic."

Polytonality

Polytonal Harmony can be either tonal or modular. In polytonality, multiple key centers are built up at a given time. This can happen tonally, as when more than one note is utilized as a focal point of gravity, or it tends to be finished with modular Harmony when more than one mode is used at once. In either case, the coming about Harmony is intricate and regularly very noisy.

Atonal Harmony

In atonal Harmony, there is no key focus. This music, promoted in the West in the twentieth century by arrangers, for example, Arnold Schoenberg and Anton Von Webern, regards each of the 12 tones just as they were focuses on gravity. The benefit is given to tones, not as they connect with some key focus, yet as they associate with each other. This music is frequently challenging to tune in; however, some of it is very beautiful.

CONCLUSION

his book provided an introduction to studying music. It took you through a series of exercises created to develop your approach to study and to learn at a distance and helped to improve your confidence as an independent learner.

Congrats!! You have completed your journey through music theory. Before the finish of this course, ideally, you will have a strong establishment of essential music terms and methods and how to play the piano. Continue practicing, and you may gain some new useful knowledge without fail.

CPSIA information can be obtained
at www.ICGtesting.com
Printed in the USA
LVHW050746291120
672741LV00010B/596

9 781801 233262